Lessons from Wednesday

Ayanna Castro

Lessons from Wednesday by Ayanna Castro

Published by Ayanna Castro
Laurel, MD
Email: ayanna@ayannacastro.com
Website: ayannacastro.com
Editor: Laura Charles-Horne

ISBN
9781691233113

DEDICATION

They are an equal split of me. The quiet introvert that enjoys her own company and the extrovert that enjoys making everyone else laugh. May their memories of me be filled with laughter, happiness and some hard truths. As their mother, it's not my job to sugar coat the world for them but prepare them to conquer it.

For Taylor and Shelby

Table of Contents

CHAPTER 1

New Opportunities and Exploiting Challenges

At the beginning of a new year, many people go through the process of coming up with New Year's resolutions and goals they want to accomplish during that year. I do not wait until January 1 to do something brand new. My birthday is the catalyst for my new year. It's when I review everything that happened over the past year and strategize how I am going to accomplish the next set of goals. My point is, you don't need a calendar to tell you when to set your goals. For you, it might be the first weekend of Spring.

Have you given some thought to some goals that you want to accomplish over the course of the year? Have you given some thought to some ways that you can improve upon or expand what you did last year? If you did something great, can you make it magnificent? Did you take time to write down a list of gratitude for the previous year? Did you take time to think about your blessings? Now, take that piece of gratefulness into the next year and think about what you can expand on to be greater.

One of my biggest opportunities was my first international speaking engagement. I was beyond excited for several reasons, but the main reason was that it was a huge personal stretch goal. I still do not know what doors will open from that initial engagement, but I can tell you I am open to every single one.

When you are faced with new opportunities, do you approach them with the intention to be successful? There is nothing worse than being given an opportunity and then half-assing it through the door. Either walk through the door saying, "Ta-dah! I'm here!" or do not walk through it at all because there is somebody else who's waiting and preparing for that very same opportunity. Speak out to the universe and say, "I'm open for my gifts and for my talents to be used."

Everybody faces challenges, right? Sometimes, the challenges can make you ready to throw in the towel and say, "To heck with it. I'm not dealing with it anymore. I'm done!" But think about the challenges from a different perspective, one of exploitation. I need you to exploit your challenges so that they turn and benefit your personal and/or professional growth.

I worked four years on a single project. It was a very long haul. As the project neared launch, I was excited and nervous. During the final meetings, one of my project team members would say, "It's all over but the shout." The plans were done, the calendar was set and I had been planning my little tail off, implementing and troubleshooting. I did all I could do to stay on top of the project. Did challenges come? Yes. Did I exploit them to no end, so that I came out of the experience even better? Absolutely!

The challenges you face are not to break you but to strengthen you. Do not look at a challenge and ask, "Oh, my God, why me?" When you are in the midst of a challenge, it is very difficult to think that everything is going to be okay when your resolve is being tested. However, when you are able to look at a challenge in the face and say, "Oh, that all you got?" it builds your confidence and character.

I hope that you are planning something absolutely and extraordinarily great. It is a time for new opportunities. If you're faced with a new opportunity, face it wholeheartedly and open to the entire experience. Do not adopt the "Well, maybe I may try it" mentality. Be completely ready and exploit your challenges to your good. Will it hurt? Maybe. Challenges by nature are a pain in the butt and inconvenient. However, sometimes your challenges are self-inflicted because you have not listened to the little birdie. Self-correct and exploit your challenges for your good.

Current Opportunities

_____

_____

_____

_____

_____

_____

_____

_____

_____

_____

_____

_____

_____

_____

_____

_____

_____

_____

_____

_____

_____

_____

_____

_____

Current Challenges

_____

_____

_____

_____

_____

_____

_____

_____

_____

_____

_____

_____

_____

_____

_____

_____

_____

_____

_____

_____

_____

_____

What is your plan to exploit your current opportunities and challenges?

Opportunity/Challenge #1

_____

_____

_____

_____

_____

Opportunity/Challenge #2

_____

_____

_____

_____

_____

Opportunity/Challenge #3

_____

_____

_____

_____

_____

CHAPTER 2

My Sister's Keeper

There are some lessons I've learned by being surrounded by some of the amazing women in my sorority. One lesson was the result of a dinner organized by my chapter to celebrate our sorority's Founder's Day. The organizers for the dinner anticipated about maybe 30 members and over 50 showed up.

On the outset and honestly quite selfishly, I thought "Oh my God, these people didn't RSVP? They didn't say they were coming. This is going to be tight." Was the space tight? Yeah, a little bit. But the experience led to a series of profound lessons I learned as I looked around the room and ear-hustled on several conversations.

Be Ready to Receive More

Many of us become stagnant with the thought of, "Well, this is good. This is enough. This makes me happy." Always be prepared to receive more. The more may come with more responsibility, but be ready to receive the abundance that comes to you whether you expect it or not. The initial shock of more people arriving wore off quickly. We were genuinely happy to see every single woman who walked through the door.

When There's Wisdom in the Room, Seek It Out

My sorority lovingly recognizes members who have celebrated 50 years of membership. These women are phenomenal in their own right. They have stories that will make you want to literally sit at their feet and listen to them for hours. It is amazing, not just from a sorority perspective, but from being a woman. The challenges that they have faced, the things that they have gone through, and the accomplishments that they've made in spite of the challenges. Those are the type of women that you want to sit around and talk to. There were two of them in the room during dinner that night; and it was just amazing to sit there and listen to them. When wisdom is in the room, seek it out. You will not always be the smartest person in the room; and if you are, you need to be in a different room. If you are the smartest person out of your crew, you need a different crew. You need to seek out the wisdom and oddly enough, wisdom doesn't always come with age.

I've often said that on your board of directors, you need to have somebody who's a decade older than you and a decade younger than you. If they're a decade older than you, they have been there, done that, got the T-shirt and the key chain. If they're younger than you, they can look at your current perspective and remind you that it doesn't have to be that difficult. Something about somebody being 10 years younger than you, but they can really look through and cut through all the minutiae of the stuff and just get to the heart of the matter. So, wisdom doesn't always come from age. Sometimes, wisdom comes from the experience of doing.

Laughter is Good for the Soul

Sometimes, the stress of being a woman can be debilitating. It can be too much to continue to wear the "mask." We wear the mask as we tell two big lies, "Everything is okay" and "Everything is fine." Let's be honest. That's a bunch of B and S. Sometimes, everything ain't great. Sometimes, everything ain't wonderful. Sometimes, things are not glorious. No, this smile that I'm wearing is not real. It is as fake as cubic zirconia.

But that night in the midst of my sorors, I heard more laughter than anything else. Laughter is good for the soul. If you are around a bunch of women and your face is still looks as if you have been sucking on lemons or if you're still rolling your eyes and sucking your teeth and can't wait to get out of the room, you are around the wrong type of women. Women have an innate ability to lift each other up. We are indeed our sister's keeper. We have the power to encourage each other better than anyone else. I'm not taking anything away from the men because I have some great men in my life who encourage me almost daily. However, women have a way of getting me to focus. Sometimes, you have to let go of the stress to allow yourself to be happy, even if you're happy for that moment. The women in the room were dealing with some personal disappointments. I was ecstatic to see them smiling and laughing and giggling. It sounded like a sorority house in the restaurant last night and it was awesome. It was good for my soul and my spirit.

Be Adaptable

This lesson was huge for me because I'm still working on it. As I mentioned earlier, only 30 people were anticipated and 50 showed up. Everyone had to be adaptable...the attendees, the organizers and the owners of the restaurant. The restaurant continued to bring tables and chairs into the room. There were two members of the chapter who took charge and made sure that the evening went as smoothly as possible. The rest of the attendees made accommodations where necessary.

When there's a situation where you have to adapt, there will always be one or two people in the room who will assess the situation and then go about the business of making things better. Those people are the people who, 9 times out of 10, have that wisdom that I was talking about a little while ago. Those are the people who add to your, "I'm okay with what I have." And give you more.

They helped the wait staff hand out food and drinks. They stepped in and became the keepers for all 50 of us that was there. I don't think any of us that attended dinner that night left feeling anything other than elated. We were with our sisters and had enjoyed a great dinner and even better conversation. It was a wonderful time had by all.

Always be ready to accept more. Be ready to accept abundance. Be ready to accept the wisdom from others. Be ready to let your stress go and just laugh. Get the giggles in. You know, seven giggles a day will make your day go a lot faster. And be adaptable. Always be ready to step in and assist where needed.

Think about the last time you were in the company of some extraordinary people. What lessons did you take away from that day? How can you apply it to your everyday interactions?

_____

_____

_____

_____

_____

_____

_____

_____

_____

_____

_____

_____

_____

_____

_____

_____

_____

_____

CHAPTER 3

Black Card Credit vs. Prepaid Debit Card Privileges

In the past, I have talked about making people pay full price for access to different facets of your life. However, some folks still do not get it; and I feel as if I need to put it in some kind of analogy so people can really understand it. And the best way is the universal language of money. Let me break this down to you in terms of credit. Some of y'all are extending Black Card privileges to people who have only earned prepaid debit cards. Let that sink in for a minute. While that sinks in, I will share some information about one of the most famous Black Cards. First of all, you must be invited to apply. Second, if you receive an invitation, you have already been approved. How? Because they have already looked at your expenditures and payment history for all of your other accounts and they know that you have spent and paid off roughly a half a million dollars over the course of one calendar year. If you are accepted, there is an initiation fee, as well as an annual fee, that will cost you around ten thousand dollars. Hefty fees aside, the perks are what makes this card worth having. Instant upgrades for travel, member-only access to major events, such as Coachella or the Grand Prix de Monaco. Not to mention the 24-hours a day, 365-days a year concierge that can do anything from research and book trips of a lifetime. Do you see how membership has its privileges?

Now think about this. There is somebody in your life who you have consistently extended credit. You have even increased their credit limit. You've allowed them to make purchases. You've allowed them to be late on their payments. And... you haven't charged them interest. You haven't cut their card off. You have allowed them to act as if the access to you, the credit in your life, is limitless. Remember, what you allow will continue. Here is where the little birdie comes in. The little birdie is a little voice in your subconscious that says, "That's cold. That's hot. They're crazy. That's dangerous." It triggers the feeling that something does not feel right. It is the nagging feeling that reminds you, you have been here before; or you have had this experience before. Why do you think you're going to have a different outcome? Most people do not listen to the little birdie.

The little birdie is not there to say, "I told you so." It is a safeguard for yourself. If you repeatedly find yourself in the same unfavorable situation with the same person, why do you continue to put yourself in that position? If you have the memory of them hurting you, if you have the memory of them consistently showing that they do not deserve the present of your presence, why do you continue to let them in? You are far too valuable for that.

As a recovering people pleaser, trust me, I get it. However, if they have shown themselves not to value who you are or what you bring to the table, why are you still inviting them to eat? Let me be very clear, I know many women, when asked, "What do you bring to the table?" their response is an immediate, "Honey, I bought the table." They bought the table, the restaurant, the building, and the block it's on. They bought it all, but they still people please. They want to make sure people aren't upset or disappointed.

Here is my question to those women. How many more times are you going to allow people to pull credit from you at the detriment to yourself? It is wonderful to help and support others but a great measure of someone's character is to say, "While I appreciate you want to do this for me, I cannot in good conscience accept it because it will be a detriment to you." If you do not have people like that in your life, then you need a new circle of friends. True friends respect your limits as well. Stop giving people Black Card privileges when they have only earned prepaid debit cards credit.

Listen to the little birdie. It will help you to remember and be mindful. I am not telling you to hold a grudge. But I am talking about you being in a situation where a person has consistently shown that they do not appreciate you, they do not value you and they do not respect you. If they have consistently done that, then you need to re-evaluate why it is you consistently let them into your space. This applies to your spouse, family, co-workers, the people within the organizations in which you affiliate, and all of the different facets of your life. You have to keep things in balance.

At this point, you could be saying, "Oh my gosh, she is just beating a dead horse." Maybe. But I never want anyone to feel like they are being taken advantage of for their kindness. There are some people with really big, generous hearts - humongous hearts. When you have a generous and benevolent heart, you need to learn how to limit the access people have to you. When you change your mind set about how you want to be treated and what you will allow, you won't have to vocalize it. Your energy will be different. The most powerful statement you can make is made in silence. When you consciously decide "I'm not going to deal with this anymore," you don't have to tell the other person that you're sick of their nonsense. Notification is not required. As your mindset shifts, so will everything else. It is amazing that when you shift your mindset, how people fall off and just drift away. And it is not because you are being "brand new" because you have an attitude or you are treating them any different. It is because you have decided in your mind, "You know what, I'm done with extending that level of credit. I'm done with that. I deserve more. I deserve somebody who's actually going to genuinely care about me."

Here is another caveat to determine if privileges need to be revoked. It is fabulous to have people that clap for you and say, "Woo hoo! Bravo!" It is great to have people cheer you on when you have a great accomplishment. But what about, "Girl, I'm just glad you got out of bed today and got some coffee. Are you okay?" It is the difference between the gutter and the glitter. If they cannot be there as you go through the gutter, what makes you think that they should have access to the glitter?

I know what it feels like to want to do it all for everybody, but you cannot do anything for anybody until you take care of yourself. And taking care of yourself includes monitoring the amount of credit that you extend. You have to monitor it. Check extended accounts and make the necessary adjustments to the credit line.

Time to re-evaluate the "lines of credit" you have extended. Make a list of everyone who has credit and determine if their current level of credit (access to you) is mutually beneficial.

_____

_____

_____

_____

_____

_____

_____

_____

_____

_____

_____

_____

_____

_____

_____

_____

_____

_____

_____

_____

_____

_____

CHAPTER 4

Being a Superhero is Overrated

A lot of what I share starts from different conversations I've had in a variety of settings. Sometimes, it's at work. Sometimes, it's with my family. Sometimes, it's within my sorority, with my friends, or with my personal board of directors. Either way, most of the topics I write or speak about is because of conversations from different areas of my life and how they seem to be talking about the same thing.

One topic that repeatedly pops up is the superhero syndrome that we perpetuate. First things first. We need to get out of our own way. When you were a child, you had absolutely no problem asking for and accepting help. If your favorite toy was on the top shelf and you couldn't reach it, you would ask until somebody came help you get your favorite toy off the top shelf. If you had fallen and scraped your knee, you would run to your mom or your dad or whoever the adult was in the room to kiss the boo-boo. With that being 100% true, please explain to me why when we become adults and contributors to society, start paying taxes, punching a clock and having real responsibilities, like mortgages, car notes, insurance and all that good stuff, we decide we no longer need help? Why do we think that we no longer need assistance?

I once read a quote that said, "If you have to wonder if you're worth more, than you already know the answer." If you're wondering, "Am I walking around with a cape on my back?" you already know have a cape on your back. If you're wondering if you have taken on too much at work, you probably need to sit down and have a conversation with your supervisor. If you think that every time you turn around and someone asks something, you're the first one to raise your hand and say, "I'll help you," perhaps...just maybe...you need to take a minute to re-evaluate what on Earth is driving you to have this superhero syndrome.

Being a superhero is overrated. You fight the battles of others, saving cats from trees and people from burning cars. You go home battered and bruised and wake up the next morning with bruises all over your body. And I'm not even talking about the physical bruises. I'm talking about the emotional bruises that you carry with you from other people's baggage. Emotional baggage can weigh and hurt more than the cuts and scars.

Like picking up pieces of glass, picking up the pieces of someone else's broken mess destroys your hands and your fingers are constantly getting bloodied. If the image is too graphic for you, that is my intention. Your hands were created to do something wonderful and great. Who is putting the bandages on your hands so that you can heal?

Being a superhero doesn't make you a better person, but it does deplete you of the energy that you need to be absolutely extraordinary. My good friend, Kemetia Foley (@adminrenegade) has always been transparent about the need for self-care and sharing how she practices it regularly. One of the ways she practices self-care is taking an hour or two in the morning for herself and starting her workday later in order to get her mind right for projects she works on. There's nothing wrong with taking a couple of extra minutes to clear your mind so that you can focus later.

There are different facets of your life and you might not realize you have a cape for each one.

"Sure, I can take that on. No problem. I can stop by the dry cleaners and the supermarket and pick the kids up from after care... Sure, I can do that".

"Yes, I'll take the lead on this project."

"Sure! I would love to be the chair of the fundraising committee."

You need to figure out how to take the capes off. Are you willing to admit that you are wearing multiple capes for work, home, kids' activities, organizations and another one for the church? You are switching capes so much, that you don't have an opportunity to just be. Worse yet, you don't take the opportunity to accept help. When did accepting help become unacceptable? When did asking for help become profanity? We might be the shot callers at work, rising through the ranks within our different organizations and we may hold powerful positions in the church and in the community, but when you lay your head down at the end of the day and all you can do is say, "I'm glad I survived!" I need you to re-evaluate your day.

You only have 168 hours in the week and tracking your 168 will show you exactly where you are spending time. I challenge you to track your 168 for one week. Color code your activities. Everything that you do for everybody else or doesn't benefit you in any way, I want you to put it in an obnoxious color that you don't like. Everything that gives you joy, everything that makes you a better person, everything that puts a smile on your face, everything that fuels you to be the extraordinary person you were created to be, put that in your favorite color.

I want you to be honest with yourself. I will tell you this right now. The first time you complete a 168 assessment is an "amen" or "ouch" moment because you will get to see for yourself how much time you're actually giving up to somebody or something else.

Being a superhero doesn't make you any greater. We've established that, right? Asking for help does not mean that you're weak, incapable of doing the job or not qualified for the position. I know plenty of people who have said, "Give me a call if you need anything" and not mean a single word of it. You need genuine people in your life because those are the people who are going to offer you genuine help. I'll give you a quick example. When I was writing my first book, my laptop gave up the holy ghost and died. My next-door neighbor, stoop therapist and my sister from somebody else gave me her old laptop. Old meaning it was still operating, she just didn't use it. But her help didn't stop there, she also offered to watch my girls, so that I could have quality writing time. Because I wasn't accustomed to 1. asking for help and 2. accepting help, I said, "No, no that's okay. That's alright. That's okay. No, I got it." several times. Finally, she got sick and tired of my self-imposed shenanigans and said, "Look, you have to finish this book. Send the girls over here. We'll l pop some popcorn and watch some movies. You take this laptop and you go write." That's what I did and I finished the book in four months.

There's nothing wrong with accepting help. There's nothing wrong with saying, "Hey, I'm drowning here." I would rather ask for help than to be in flames and burning while somebody is standing right there with a water hose.

My mother raised me to be independent, so I have a very difficult time asking for help. I've always figured out how to make it happen. If there's a problem, give me a second because I got a plan B, C, D and all the way through Z. I'm Ms. Work Your Package, Ms. Chief Maven, and Ms. I Got It All Together.

So, if I'm telling you that it is okay to ask for help, guess what? It is okay to ask for help! Sometimes, people know you need help, but they wait because they don't want to be bossy, intrusive or step on your toes. They understand you're prideful and you're not going to ask for the help. They're waiting. They already know you need help when they say, "Hey, I see you're having difficulty with this. Let me help you with this." or "Hey, what are you working on? I'm really interested in that. Let me see what you're working on." Your board of directors is listening to you. They know your pain points and what triggers them. When someone on your board of directors asks, "Hey, do you need some help?" I need you to be honest. Stop going around picking up all these broken pieces of everybody else and keeping your hands bloodied. Your fingerprints are almost gone. Your identity is almost gone because you're so busy picking up these broken pieces of glass for everybody else and you're not taking care of yourself.

168 Tracker and Assessment – Use the trackers on the following pages to help you see where you are spending your time. Anything that benefits you, highlight in your favorite color. At the end of the week, take a hard look at where you spend most of your time and determine where your time would be better spent.

Here are some suggestions of how to categorize your time for easy computing of your total hours.

Activity

Sleep

Work

Commute

Social Media

TV

Reading

Time with family

Time with friends

Volunteering

Exercise

Household chores

Miscellaneous

SUNDAY			
12AM		**12PM**	
1AM		**1PM**	
2AM		**2PM**	
3AM		**3PM**	
4AM		**4PM**	
5AM		**5PM**	
6AM		**6PM**	
7AM		**7PM**	
8AM		**8PM**	
9AM		**9PM**	
10AM		**10PM**	
11AM		**11PM**	

MONDAY			
12AM		**12PM**	
1AM		**1PM**	
2AM		**2PM**	
3AM		**3PM**	
4AM		**4PM**	
5AM		**5PM**	
6AM		**6PM**	
7AM		**7PM**	
8AM		**8PM**	
9AM		**9PM**	
10AM		**10PM**	
11AM		**11PM**	

TUESDAY			
12AM		**12PM**	
1AM		**1PM**	
2AM		**2PM**	
3AM		**3PM**	
4AM		**4PM**	
5AM		**5PM**	
6AM		**6PM**	
7AM		**7PM**	
8AM		**8PM**	
9AM		**9PM**	
10AM		**10PM**	
11AM		**11PM**	

WEDNESDAY

12AM		**12PM**	
1AM		**1PM**	
2AM		**2PM**	
3AM		**3PM**	
4AM		**4PM**	
5AM		**5PM**	
6AM		**6PM**	
7AM		**7PM**	
8AM		**8PM**	
9AM		**9PM**	
10AM		**10PM**	
11AM		**11PM**	

THURSDAY			
12AM		12PM	
1AM		1PM	
2AM		2PM	
3AM		3PM	
4AM		4PM	
5AM		5PM	
6AM		6PM	
7AM		7PM	
8AM		8PM	
9AM		9PM	
10AM		10PM	
11AM		11PM	

FRIDAY

12AM		12PM	
1AM		1PM	
2AM		2PM	
3AM		3PM	
4AM		4PM	
5AM		5PM	
6AM		6PM	
7AM		7PM	
8AM		8PM	
9AM		9PM	
10AM		10PM	
11AM		11PM	

SATURDAY

12AM		**12PM**	
1AM		**1PM**	
2AM		**2PM**	
3AM		**3PM**	
4AM		**4PM**	
5AM		**5PM**	
6AM		**6PM**	
7AM		**7PM**	
8AM		**8PM**	
9AM		**9PM**	
10AM		**10PM**	
11AM		**11PM**	

How did you do? Are you satisfied with how you spent your time? Were you more mindful of how you spent your time knowing you were tracking it?

Activity	Total Hours
Sleep	
Work	
Commute	
Social Media	
TV	
Reading	
Time with family	
Time with friends	
Volunteering	
Exercise	
Household chores	
Miscellaneous	

CHAPTER 5

Self-Care Isn't Selfish

A lot of people think that self-care falls in the realm of your emotional self-care. However, self-care falls into three different categories: emotional, mental and physical.

I'll start with the physical first. Physical self-care is simply taking care of yourself physically. Are you getting enough sleep? Are you resting? Are you listening to your body when it says, "I need to rest?" Are you giving your body the rest that it needs to recuperate, regenerate, rejuvenate, to be ready for the next day? Or do you stay on full tilt? If you're one of those people that stay on "ready, set..." and always prepared for "go," you have to give your body some rest. Are you listening to the signals that your body is giving you?

For me, I know that if the barometric pressure drops too low, I will get a migraine. I'm mindful of that. Sometimes, I have to schedule my day around the weather. Imagine that. If you know that you have a tendency to be exhausted in the evening, don't agree to do a conference call at nine o'clock. Know your ebbs and flows. Know what you need to do. Know how you need to manage your body. Knowing when to say "no" to additional responsibilities is key.

Mental health is also part of self-care. What are you taking in or listening to? What are you putting into your mind? What are you saying to yourself? I am an empath, which basically means I physically take on the emotions and the stresses that are around me. I am very clear about the energy that is in the room and what type of energy someone has around me. My family, particularly my daughters, will watch to see if I'm reserving myself from anyone and then govern themselves accordingly. If your energy is off, you can't be next to me because I absorb all of that whether I'm having a direct conversation or not. Mannerisms, actions or the way someone speaks to or treats someone else, still impact me. I'm cautious about what I read. I'm cautious about what I listen to. You have to be cognizant of yourself and your needs even from a mental standpoint.

What are you doing to practice self-care? Are you scheduling time for yourself? Are you blocking out 10 minutes for yourself? One of my really good girlfriends and a member of my board of directors told me, "You need to take at least an hour for yourself every day." I responded, "Do you realize I have two kids, a husband, a dog, and a whole bunch of stuff on my plate? I don't have a full hour to take for myself every day." She said, "Well then start with 10 minutes." You need time for yourself. You have to schedule time for yourself. You have to make time, even if you have to put it in your planner. Set a reminder on your phone." If you're working at a stressful job, schedule 10 minutes every other hour to walk away and to give yourself that time to breath and recollect yourself.

You have to maintain boundaries because you teach people how to treat you. For example, if you always pick up the phone for non-emergencies, available for last minute meetings or saying "yes" when you truthfully want to say "Hell no," you are teaching people how to treat you. Every time you agree to do something that depletes you without you speaking up for yourself, you reinforce the notion that your self-care is not important. It is your responsibility to teach others your self-care is important. If they don't see you taking care of you, they will not be inclined to help you take care of yourself.

The women that I roll with, the people who are in my crew, the people who are on my board of directors, the chicks that I look up to, run some hectic schedules. We work the hell out of these 168 hours. When I asked them how do they manage self-care, here are some of the tips they shared:

- Listen to your body. If you ignore it, it will force you to rest.
- Set boundaries with your time and energy.
- Utilize technology to manage your 168.
- It's not a once-a-year time of thing. Take a few moments every day. It's not about the two-week vacation.
- Take off or schedule mental health days.
- "No" is a complete sentence.
- Place buffers in in your schedule so that you don't have back-to-back meetings.
- Get to know yourself and your triggers.
- Put yourself on a time out before you burn out.

- Pushing through when you should rest is the worst thing you can do to yourself and others. The result of pushing through is being cranky, getting sick and things in your life falling apart.
- Remove the emotional leeches from your life...even if it's a family member.

Make a list of the things you will and will not do to practice self-care:

_____

_____

_____

_____

_____

_____

_____

_____

_____

_____

_____

_____

_____

_____

_____

_____

_____

_____

_____

_____

_____

_____

_____

_____

_____

_____

_____

_____

CHAPTER 6

The Road to Excellence is Never Easy, but It is Worth It

In 2018, I had the opportunity to speak in London at the Executive Secretary LIVE Conference. In the weeks leading up to the conference, I was excited to be traveling to London, but also to be among some amazing trainers as well as women and men seeking both professional and personal development. It was amazing to take the message and brand of Work Your Package™ global. During my visit to Abu Dhabi and Dubai the previous year, I said, "Lord, if you want me to continue to take this message worldwide, I'm willing. If you want it to be global, I'm willing."

I didn't know what opportunities would present themselves after London. But I did know there was a palpable energy that I felt in the weeks and days leading up to my departure flight. I was excited because it was an opportunity for me to do what it is that I was called to do. It was an opportunity for me to speak to the heart of women (and a few men) because I know that is my purpose. That is my rent here on Earth. I knew that it was a chance for me to grow.

To be perfectly honest, speaking on an international stage is far different than speaking on a stage that you created because you are the host for the event. I appreciated the stellar organization of the entire conference and the attention to the smallest details. It was truly a world-class experience. There were 200 delegates from all around the world in attendance. I was excited, scared, nervous and ready all at the same time. In preparation for the conference, I did an edit, revamp and reprint of my first book, *Work Your Package: The Guide to Being the Total Package*. The joy of being self-published is that you can do a lot of things yourself. You pretty much work against a deadline you've set for yourself and work at your leisure. Well, working "at my leisure" led me to work until 1:30am one night revamping the book. And guess what? I did not complain when the alarm clock went off because I was doing what was needed...for me and my brand. The women and men who attended the conference deserved to get 100 percent of the Work Your Package™ experience and that's what I delivered.

I share this with you because I want you to understand that whatever your goal is for excellence and being absolutely extraordinary, the road ahead might look very difficult but at the very end of it all, it is worth it.

You will face challenges as you strive towards your goal, whether it's a stretch or growth goal. You will face people who told you in the beginning, "I have your back", but when you needed them, they were nowhere to be found. Some will claim to have your back, but they don't. You will face people who will tell you flat out "you can't do it." It's all part of the journey. I'm thankful that I have people who say, "Go, Ayanna go!" I'm thankful for the people to say, "Girl, you got it." And I'm thankful for the people who ask incredulously about my goals as if it's an impossibility.

The road to being extraordinary can be tiring. You must schedule time for yourself when you're in the midst of being absolutely phenomenal, fantastic, amazing and rocking it out on all cylinders. Take time to celebrate how far you've come instead focusing on what hasn't been accomplished.

I speak to the heart of women. I know that I speak to women that are like me. Whether it's a corporate gig and you have a passion that won't let you rest until you feed it or you're a full-time entrepreneur and you're out there every day making sure things happen. I understand and I get it. My purpose here is to serve you and to share a little piece of my journey, my triumphs and even some of my challenges because it is not all roses.

It is not always perfect or fit in a box with a nice little bow on top. But at the end of it all, know your goal is worth the sacrifices.

CHAPTER 7

Self-Love

Carolyn Kirk once said, "Self-Love requires you to be honest about your current choices and thought patterns and undertake new practices that reflect self-worth."

Are you taking care of yourself and practicing self-love? You might say, "Well, I love myself. I love me better than anybody else can love me." people continue to watch you being taken advantage of by others who don't deserve the level of access that you have given them. You're not doing what is required to be honest about loving yourself. Are you waiting for other people to love you? Are you waiting for other people to show you that you are worthy of love? Guess what? You're already worthy of that love. You already have it in you to love yourself. When I speak about having everything you already need to be extraordinary, I also believe that everyone has it within them to find a way to love themselves.

I had a conversation with a couple of girlfriends once and we talked about how we all struggle with insecurities. We shared how we still struggle at times with speaking up for ourselves. The conversation eventually led to the different ways we don't love on ourselves. We talked about something as small as giving ourselves a compliment. When was the last time you looked in the mirror and complimented yourself? Self-love starts with you. If you're looking for people to love you the way you require and the way you deserve, you have to show them.

The caveat to that is sometimes people will come along in your life who will love you beyond what you think you are worth and you will struggle with it. You will fight it. You will deny it. You will ask questions and you will be cynical about it. But the fact is, some people will come into your life to love you just because you're you. Some people will love you despite yourself. Some people will continue to love you even after, as my grandmother would say, "You done shown your entire tail to everybody." If you have somebody who has come into your life and loves you beyond what you believe that you are worth, ask them "Why are you so good to me?" You will probably be surprised by the response. Listen to them. Maybe they see something in you that you don't. Maybe they see something that was once there, but now they see that you've lost your way and they're trying to help you get back on track. Maybe it's because they see a diamond in the rough. Maybe it's because they see all those jagged pieces and they have the ability to smooth it out for you.

If you are struggling to love yourself, allow someone who wants to love you to do so. Love does not always have to come in physical form. It is not just romantic love that says, "I'm here. I'm listening. What do you need? How can I help you? Is there anything that you need help with?" Love can come from a member of your board of directors who is watching you struggle with a project and asks, "Can I take this task off your plate?"

Love yourself without waiting for somebody else to give you a reason or to make you feel like you have to have a reason to love yourself. Self-love should not be predicated on what others think of you, nor should it be predicated on your past mistakes.

How will you show yourself love? How will you teach others to love you?

_____

_____

_____

_____

_____

_____

_____

_____

_____

_____

_____

_____

_____

_____

_____

_____

_____

_____

_____

_____

_____

CHAPTER 8

Wisdom Comes at a Cost

I remember a conversation with a newer member of my board of directors. They mentioned that prior to really getting to know me, they watched my live social media posts and came to the conclusion that people can't give the that type of commentary, advice or insight without living through something. At first, I thought, "They are just blowing smoke. That was just something nice to say." They went on to say how very impressed they were on how I was willing to be transparent.

Truth is, I know a lot of people who have gone through some really traumatic things and they have yet to be transparent, but their wisdom shows up in different ways. They are people who are usually the calm in the midst of the storm when something catastrophic happens. They tend to be stoic and may appear to be very standoffish, but they have the ability to selflessly work with people who experience a similar trauma.

They have gone through situations so traumatic that when they share their story, the response is usually, "Oh my God, I can't believe you live through that." Those people have this kind of built-in type of wisdom that you can't get from a textbook or any psychology book. You can't read about that type of wisdom anywhere. When people say, "That was so insightful." understand that they not only respect your wisdom, but they also appreciate knowing there's a backstory behind that wisdom.

I often talk about being transparent and I think about someone who I've been asking to write a book for years. Very early on in our friendship, he told me just a little bit of his story. I asked him when he was going to write his life story and he said, and I quote, "I'm too young for that maybe in 20 years." My response was "You don't know what tomorrow has for you. And who says you're going to be here in 20 years? Instead of holding onto your story and not sharing it, you could be helping God knows how many other people. You're impacting people one by one when you can be impacting the masses with your story." He didn't have an immediate witty response, which let me know I struck a nerve and he knew I was telling the truth.

Your wisdom came at a cost, but it's worth sharing. The wisdom that you gain from your life experiences, heartaches and hardships are not to break you. It's to make you stronger. And as you get stronger, you are then able to impart that wisdom to somebody else. Have you ever been in a situation where you can see the road that this person is getting ready to head down and you were able to just say, "Wait a minute, don't do it."? You don't say it in a "know-it-all" type of way, but as a "Baby, I've been there, done that and have a tee shirt" type of way. I've had conversations like that with other women about the things that I've gone through. Battling infertility for years, having two babies back-to-back while working full-time, then losing a job, losing a grandmother and my father's murder happened all in two weeks. I am able to have that conversation from a place of wisdom.

There's a difference between eyewitness and life witness wisdom. Life witness wisdom holds far more weight than somebody telling you, "Oh, I read somewhere that in order to get over the grief of significant loss, you should..." (Insert eye roll here) Did you live it? Here's another thing, wisdom does not come with age. Wisdom comes through experiences. The wisdom that you gain from experiences can be imparted to anybody at any age and you can gain that wisdom at any time. Think about the time that you touched something for the first time and it was hot and you burned your hand. You were probably pretty young, right? I bet you were able to tell your little brother or sister, "Don't touch that. That's hot. It burned me." That's wisdom you were able to share to keep your sibling from getting hurt...you were a child. Think about the time when you disobeyed your parents and missed curfew. What happened the next time you were able to go out after you were no longer grounded? Your friends wanted to hang out a little bit longer and you said, "No, because last time we did that, I got grounded." I've met some real inept and narrow-minded 50-year-olds who have nothing to offer. In their view, the situation didn't provide lesson so they won't share it. The worst thing that you could do is be stingy with your wisdom. Why would you let somebody else go through what you've gone through without sharing how you overcame it?

Wisdom comes at a cost. It's not going to be pretty or easy. You're going to cry and you're going to hurt. You're going to want to throw things, cuss, fuss and scream. But at the end of it, all the wisdom that you gain is worth it. I would not exchange a single tear, panic attack or anxiety attack. I wouldn't exchange a single time that I've had to get rushed to the hospital because I thought I was having a heart attack. I would not exchange any of those experiences because I know the wisdom that I gained was for as much as I may love other people, I love me so much more; and if I do not love me first and take care of myself, I cannot possibly love anybody else.

Don't think about your current situation as a negative. If you are in a bad situation right now, think of it as a training day. It might turn into training week, training month or training year. For some of us, our training is lengthy. So much so that you may really want to have a conversation with God. *Like really? Is this what we're going to do? I'm still going through this? I do not have the patience of Job, this is ridiculous. I am still going through this Lord?* But then you come through it and you're able to tell the masses what they are going through is worth the journey and the wisdom that they will gain from it is priceless.

I encourage you not to be selfish with your experiences, but also to be careful with how you share your story. I am a huge fan of Dr. Brene Brown. Her studies reveal that being vulnerable is very hard to do because there is shame wrapped up in that vulnerability. You have to be careful with whom you share your story because not everyone can bear the weight. There are certain people I know I can tell them anything. There's nothing I can tell them that will make them clutch their proverbial pearls and say, "Girl, I can't deal with you no more."

Then, there are some who said they could handle it, were tested and failed miserably. It wasn't necessarily what they said, but what I saw in their eyes that let me know they couldn't handle it. So, guess what? I still love them and they still have a certain level of access to me, but I know I can't share everything with them.

Don't be selfish with the knowledge that you gain from your painful experiences. Here's something you might not realize. All that wisdom is stored in your little birdie. You might have a temporary lapse, but your little birdie never forgets. She/he will remind you when you're about to do something that will set you up for a repeated lesson due to your self-imposed shenanigans. Sometimes, we have to go through lessons one, two, three, four or five times because the first through fourth time you really did not get the true meaning of the lesson. But by the fifth time, you finally get it. We can go through the same lesson repeatedly. Not because we're a glutton for punishment, but so that when we have finally learned the lesson, for that final time, we're then equipped and qualified to give that knowledge to somebody else. Too often, we have people in our lives who can only provide eyewitness wisdom; yet, we allow them to weigh in on major decisions. Be the person for somebody else who is equipped and qualified to give life experience wisdom.

What life-witness wisdom can you offer to someone else who is facing the same type of experience?

_____

_____

_____

_____

_____

_____

_____

_____

_____

_____

_____

_____

_____

_____

_____

_____

_____

_____

_____

_____

_____

_____

CHAPTER 9

Are You Overreacting?

A couple of years ago I did a blog post called "A Proportional Response" and I used the example of an episode of the television drama called "West Wing." The episode was about the president wanting to bomb everything to hell because of a situation that happened. He was angry and irrationally emotional. That episode has always made me think about a proportional response to conflict. Are you responding to situations in a manner that is warranted? Sometimes, we allow our feelings to take over and end up taking things personal.

I will use myself as an example. I hate being told that I'm doing something wrong. I hate being told that what I've done is displeasing to someone. I hate it with a passion. But sometimes I have to sit there and ask, "Is there any truth in it? Am I being oversensitive? Am I overreacting?" For some people, when they're told that they're wrong or something is brought to their attention, they have a tendency to immediately go nuclear to defend their position. They stand flat-footed in their conviction as to why they did what they did and how dare you question them. Then there are folks who take a minute to observe everything, think things through, figure out what was actually said and see if there's an ounce of truth to it. Some people take a moment to sit back and reflect and say, "You know what? Maybe that was out of order. Maybe that was kind of wrong. Maybe I should have responded a different way." The people who take the time to really sit back and analyze what was actually said and not take it as a personal affront are usually the people who don't overreact. If you're the type of person who immediately takes any questioning of your actions, your motives or your words personally, you are probably the person that overreacts the most.

I'll give you a perfect example. I've been told multiple times over that I stretch myself too thin. I've been told that I have my hands in everything and I don't stay still long enough to enjoy the moment. At first I wanted to explode and say, "How dare you? How dare you question my drive? How dare you question my passion? How dare you question me taking my commitments seriously? How dare you?!" I was indignant about it. But then a funny thing happened. I stopped being insulted and really thought about it. I was stretching myself too thin. I was saying "yes" where I really should have been saying, "Hell no." I took a moment to step back and said, "Why the heck am I getting so mad?" Because there's some truth in it. It wasn't an insult to my character. To be clear, you can insult just about anything about me. You can say you don't like my hair. You can say you don't like my makeup. You can say you don't like my clothes. You could say I'm too fluffy, I'm too short. You can say whatever you like, but what you can't do is insult my integrity, my work ethic or the love I have for my family and not expect a response. There are some things that are non-negotiable. Your non-negotiables are directly linked to why people admire you. However, even with your non-negotiables, I'm not saying it's okay to flip all the way out. Take a moment to not overreact. My grandmother once told me, "Everything doesn't have to be a thunderstorm. Sometimes, it can be a spring shower. Things are still going to get wet."

It makes sense, right? Are you overreacting or have you given yourself a minute to assess the situation for what it is? Are you giving yourself time to ask questions? Not asking questions can lead you to assume and automatically think the worst. And I think that's why people overreact, because they haven't taken the time to ask the question and assume the worst. Asking investigative questions will help you to not go nuclear and overreact to things that honestly don't require that type of response. To be perfectly honest, when you have a nuclear response, it makes you look unstable. It is important to be congruent with your words, actions and appearance. If you look beautiful and you speak eloquently, but flip off at people at the drop of a hat, you're not being congruent.

Think about the situations that you're in right now. You can probably think about one right now in the last 24 hours. Someone said something to you that you feel is wrong and you felt that it needed to be addressed immediately. Were you looking for correction or were you looking for crucifixion? Because if you were looking for correction, you didn't overreact. Crucifixion, however, brings out a totally different response. If you're looking for crucifixion and that's where you are most comfortable, nine times out of ten, you will repeatedly overreact to situations that only need correction.

Your mental health depends on you being able to navigate things that come your way and say, "You know what? That's really not important." It also depends on the relationship. When it's someone you care about or love, you have a tendency to listen to what they have to say. When you respect that person, you have a tendency to really think about what they said. You will govern yourself accordingly and probably won't overreact. Conversely, if you have a lack of respect for someone or if you don't really think that person is worth your time, crucifixion is probably your comfort level. Respect for a person and seeking correction will lead to you not overreacting. Having a superiority complex, believing that you're better than somebody and looking for crucifixion will make you overreact every single time.

CHAPTER 10

Focus On What Is Important

We live by "to-do" lists. We always have something to do. When someone asks, "Hey, what are you up to?" you may feel as if you're slacking if you don't have a laundry list of items. You end up saying, "Oh, I have so much to do." While you might have a lot to do, are you focusing on what is important? I'll use myself as an example. On any given Wednesday, I'll have another seven days' worth of stuff to do between then and Saturday. In the midst of the things to get done, there are non-negotiables. Come hell or high water, they must get done.

As you review your checklist, you have to look at what is really important. There are probably a bunch of things that you would like to do, but what will have the greatest impact in the long run? I've found that outsourcing tasks that can suck up a lot of your time, like grocery shopping, is a time-saver. If you are like me, you might want to select your own produce and meats, but ordering your groceries online will save you time in the long run. Outsourcing your to-do list isn't lazy. It's a smart way to manage your 168.

You may have a thousand things to do (I know I'm exaggerating, but that's how it can feel). You have people tugging at your sleeve that want your attention. You are needed in a meeting, your review is needed for a report, or they need you to write the report. The only thing you have control over is what you say "yes" to. If you already have a laundry list of things to do, take a moment, write it all out, use a mobile app or put in your calendar. I am a hybrid. I am a paper and pen type of girl. I like to write my stuff down. I like to cross things off, but I use my Outlook at work and a Google calendar at home as my backup. When I'm on the go and on the rare occasions that I don't have a pen or a paper with me or a notebook with me, I will jot something down in my phone. The trick is making sure that you have the tools that you need and that you are comfortable with.

Think about all the different things, all the different places where people demand your time and request your time. Think about that and then go from there and prioritize what is most important. You can't do everything. You can't please everybody, but you need to focus on what is important. Sometimes, the cost of being awesome and responsible is getting more responsibility. Take time to focus on what's important and everything else that isn't mission critical can wait.

CHAPTER 11

Get The Heck Out of Your Own Way

Five years prior to my first international speaking engagement, I had an idea. I had a vision for something that I wanted to do, but *Work Your Package™* as it is right now was not clear. It was about as clear as muddy water. While I was writing my first book, I was also planning my first conference. At that time, the conference consisted of a half a day of programming, a panel of speakers and some lunch. I wrapped it up with my book signing and that was it for the day. The format has changed over the years, but the purpose and focus remained the same. I created a conference and a brand to speak to the heart of women regardless of socioeconomic background or profession. We all have the same pain points and that's what I speak to.

I am blessed to have life experiences that have provided lessons I can share with others. I'm surrounded by people who continuously push me forward. The opportunity to speak in

London almost didn't happen because I never saw the first invitation from the conference producer. As fate would have it, Lucy Brazier and I attended the same conference a year later and she says, "You know, I reached out to you to speak in London in March and I never heard from you." I felt like the floor had dropped from underneath me. I had no idea that she'd sent the email because she used an email address that I rarely use. Fast-forward a year later; and I was glad that I had gotten out of my own way. I'm glad that I had enough common sense to listen to the people who constantly pushed me and told me "You can do it and you're going to be great." I'm thankful for the people who reminded me that I wasn't just *You're Work Your Package™,* but *Work Your Package™* doesn't exist without me. There are thousands of people out there that are motivational speakers and trainers. There are thousands of people out there who have written books. You can throw a penny and hit a blog. But I know that my personal experience is my own and that's what makes me unique.

What are you blocking yourself from? What are you blocking yourself from receiving? What are you talking yourself out of? What are you telling yourself you can't do? How many times have you come up with a brilliant idea and talked yourself out of it before you even took the first step? Seriously, and I say this with all the love and honey sugar booboos that I can muster up...Get the hell out of your own way! You are your worst enemy! If you don't believe me, check in with the people who love you. I guarantee that they see exactly what it is that you have to offer and how you are selfishly sitting on something that's supposed to be shared with other people. If you have something that you are passionate about, can't stop thinking about and you are wondering how you can bring it to fruition, it is probably something you need to just go ahead and do. If you are sitting there wondering if you should, the answer is probably "yes." I'm willing to bet that there is someone reading this right now who is sitting on $100, $1,000, $10,000, $100,000 or $1,000,000 ideas and they're sitting on it because they don't believe that it's worth anything. The idea you are sitting on may have a monetary value. What idea or innovative process do you have that could possibly improve your children's school or the entire school district? How can you improve the organizations that you belong to? What if you're sitting there holding on to an idea for a possible community service outreach program that can benefit hundreds of people? Don't sit there and sell yourself short. Who says that it has to be somebody else that comes up with the idea? It very well can be you. You just need to learn how to get the heck out of your own way.

Don't second guess yourself. Don't second guess your brilliance. Don't second guess your capabilities and the possibilities that can be produced from your skills. Too many of you are sleeping on them and you need to cut it out.

What are you blocking yourself from? What are you blocking yourself from receiving? What are you talking yourself out of doing? What are you telling yourself you can't do?

_____

_____

_____

_____

_____

_____

_____

_____

_____

_____

_____

_____

_____

_____

_____

_____

_____

_____

_____

_____

CHAPTER 12

You Never Know Who's Watching

You never know who's watching. You never know who's looking to see whether or not your words are congruent with your actions and that your actions are congruent with the words. You never know who is watching the replay of your social media videos or reading your blog posts months after you've already posted them. When you learn to get out of your way and stop second guessing yourself, someone will come along that will confirm and acknowledge you're on the right path.

Right now, someone is watching as you go through your journey towards being absolutely fabulous and extraordinary. Though you might hit some hiccups and some bumps along the way, someone is watching you and saying, "You know, they've really got their stuff together."

Even if you consider yourself a seasoned professional, you still have to practice your craft in order to give your best. After working with senior level executives for over 20 years, I've come to realize that if you don't still get nervous before you do something, you have become too cocky and you need to do a reset. It is very comforting to hear veteran international speakers and event hosts share that they still get nervous before they deliver their presentations. They host multiple international conferences each year and have spoken at hundreds of events to thousands of attendees; yet, they still get nervous. That piece of advice helped me to feel a little bit more confident and comfortable as I prepare for speaking engagements. That confidence allows me to give conference and event attendees 110% of the Chief Maven and Work Your Package™ experience.

You never know who's watching you. It may not be in the arena of speaking, but it could be at your job, church or with your kids. I know that my girls watch me far more than I give them credit for, which is why I do my very best to give them something positive to see. I don't sugarcoat my experiences for them. I share my struggles and when I'm feeling disappointed as well as when I'm excited and I'm elated. When I received my project management professional certification, they were excited for me because they understood the sacrifices I made to accomplish the goal.

People are watching you. How you handle your struggles, your challenges and your opportunities. Are you blowing your opportunities or are you taking advantage of them? Do you handle challenges like a petulant child? Do you blame other people for your foolishness and self-imposed shenanigans? Are you taking ownership for it? People are watching. Make sure you give them something positive and authentic to see.

If someone was to write an article about you based on how you handle challenges along your journey to being extraordinary, what would the article say?

_____

_____

_____

_____

_____

_____

_____

_____

_____

_____

_____

_____

_____

_____

_____

_____

_____

_____

_____

_____

_____

Ayanna T. Castro

CHAPTER 13

It's Not Your Fight

The people who know me well and who I consider more family than friends know that I am extraordinarily loyal and protective. Sometimes to the point where I will take on somebody else's fight. I've had to learn (multiple times and sometimes the hard way) that it's not always my fight.

While we may get upset and commiserate with the person who's going through something, we must learn it's not our fight. We have to learn how to remain in a supportive role and not step in ready for fisticuffs, whether physically or verbally. We have to learn not to throw gasoline on the fire. When you're dealing with a situation where you're watching somebody go through something that: a) you have no control over; b) they have no control over; or c) probably couldn't have been avoided - Why are you jumping into their fight?

You have to ask yourself, "What can I possibly do for them by jumping into the fight?" If you don't have any control over it, if you can't make it right, if you can't fix it, if you can't control it, have a seat. If they have no control over it or there's nothing they can do about it, have several seats.

I have a Polish proverb at my desk that says, "Every time you feel yourself being pulled into other people's drama, repeat these words...NOT MY CIRCUS, NOT MY MONKEYS." I look at daily, sometimes several times a day, because it's my nature to want to help. Here's what I realized. You cannot help everybody, especially if you're at a point where you are barely holding on yourself. If you're barely holding onto the ledge, how are you going to take your hand off the ledge to reach out to help somebody else? Get yourself together first.

Also, there's the possibility the person put themselves in the precarious situation and there's a lesson they need to learn. Lessons are often repeated and come back in different ways. Maybe it's something that their little birdie told them a long time ago and they just refuse to listen. Maybe it's something that they need to learn once and for all.

Maybe you've always jumped in to save others. I'm here to tell you...stop jumping in to save people. Stop putting your "nice" all over everything. Some people are in the situation that they're in because they put themselves there. Either they've allowed it, they didn't listen to their little birdie the first, second or third time or sometimes things just happen. As much as you want to help, be supportive. You can be their "10-minute person" (The person they can call, cry, cuss and vent...but only for 10 minutes). Be supportive without putting on armor to take on the battle for them. Some people need to do battle for themselves to learn their lesson. Some people have become so dependent and accustomed to us coming in and saving the day that they don't know how to save themselves. You did not put them in their precarious situation. Refer them to professional resources or give wise counsel without throwing gasoline on the fire, but don't be the person that always says, "I'm going to fix it." You do not know what lessons lie within the difficulties they're going through. You might be hindering their growth by wanting to step in and fix it. Think of it this way...you might be hindering the growth of somebody else because you wanted to step in and fix a situation that contains a lesson specifically for them.

If you are on the other side of this, meaning you are the one who is going through a rough patch, you might think I'm being harsh. I lovingly say this with life witness experience, not eyewitness knowledge, be thankful for every time somebody does not jump in to save you. The lessons you learn from having to deal with stuff yourself and not somebody coming in to save the day will stick with you. You will, in turn, be able to impart that life witness wisdom to someone else. The people who love you haven't abandoned you during your struggle, they may have realized there is nothing they can fix or control; and they are allowing you to go through the lesson so that you can grow and be a better version of yourself.

What fight are you currently fighting that is not your own? Why do you feel the need to be part of the fight? Is it possible you are hindering the owner of the fight from learning a valuable lesson?

_____

_____

_____

_____

_____

_____

_____

_____

_____

_____

_____

_____

_____

_____

_____

_____

_____

_____

CHAPTER 14

Knuckle Up, Buttercup

I think that we get so wrapped up in our greatness and our fantastic journey to extraordinary that we can forget that bs and shenanigans will come our way. We get so comfortable in the fanfare, congratulations and "you go girls" that we can forget we will eventually have some challenges. Sometimes, we forget the road and journey to being extraordinary will come with challenges. No one ever told any of us the journey would be easy. *Knuckle up, buttercup.* My brother would say that to me sometimes when I would get beside myself. When I thought things were too hard or were just unfair, he would just say "Okay. Knuckle up, buttercup."

Who said just because you are awesome and great and brilliant and just all around fantastic that you are impervious to a bad day? If you've never had one, then you're not living the life you're supposed to be living. If you have not had a moment where you had to say, "Oh, this is ridiculous, but I still have to keep going," then you're not doing something right. When you are doing something extraordinary, it is never going to be easy. If it comes easy, it probably won't last. If you're going through challenges in something that you were assigned or called to do, understand that you already have everything inside of you to be extraordinary. So what makes you think you don't have everything inside of you to overcome this obstacle? I need you to think about it. There's balance in that. You have everything inside of you to be extraordinary. I'm willing to bet you my favorite pair of pumps and a handbag that you already have everything inside of you to overcome any obstacle.

Knuckle up, buttercup because the journey to being extraordinary, memorable and legendary does not come without some rough patches. It does not come without disappointments and it does not come without the need to pull out to cussing spirit sometimes. The journey is not over just because you encounter an obstacle. The journey is not over because one person said, "No." The journey is not over because one person didn't have your back. The journey is not over because people didn't do what they said they were going to do or supposed to do. The journey is not over because you had a setback. Knuckle up today and get it done. Somebody is watching you. Somebody is waiting for you to be absolutely extraordinary and wonderful. They don't have time for you to be passive about being awesome.

CHAPTER 15

Progress in the Midst of Mess

Look up the word "busy" and my picture will probably be the definition. For years, I've had my hands in a lot of things and one time. I'm on the go and on the run, whether it's for my family, my job or my sorority. My girls are very active between Girls Scouts, dancing school and volunteer efforts. Their calendar often rivals my own. At work, I have the joy of producing and orchestrating great events and programs primarily focused on employee engagement. So, while I might experience the occasional anxiety about a particular task, I enjoy my job. There was a point when everything was competing for mental space. My desk at work and my desk at home looked like a hot mess. I walked around for weeks saying I felt like a hot mess. But then I thought of everything I completed and checked off on my list of tasks.

Think about the progress that you make in the midst of the mess. Laundry, cooking, redecorating a room in your home. In the midst of all that progress, there is some mess. Sometimes, you want to throw your hands up and say, "The heck with it!" but then you realize you are still getting things done. In the midst of the mess, there is progress. Don't take your eye off the fact that you are making progress and the goal you are getting closer to achieving. Don't take your eye off the fact that you have made great strides.

No matter your current "mess" (laundry or a multibillion-dollar project), you might be feeling completely overwhelmed and ready to throw in the towel. I need you to look backwards and see how far you've come because, in the midst of all of what you're dealing with...the challenges, opposition, naysayers, all of the negative Nellies and the chatty Patty's...you're STILL making progress.

There have been plenty of times when I've said to no one in particular, "The whole project can go to hell in a handbasket. The entire project. I'm ready to throw the whole thing away." Then I think about what I accomplished that day, that week and over the past month. I think about what my whiteboard looked like at the beginning of the project. I took a picture of my whiteboard once and sent it to my husband. He said, "Oh, is this for next month?" I had a huge belly laugh and told him that it was all for the following week. He made a face like he wanted to clutch his pearls. His reaction let me know that I am a badass when it comes to getting the seemingly impossible done.

Don't beat yourself up because you are not where you think you should be at the moment. Don't beat yourself up because you know you might be a little bit behind your deadline. This is for my fellow Type A folks. It's okay to give yourself just a little bit of leeway and say, "You know what? I'm not where I was and it's not going to be as long as it has been." If you are nervous because it is your first time tackling a task, it might be scary, but I believe you are up to the challenge and will learn from it. Believe that you are worth everything your heart desires. Believe that you are worth every good thing that comes your way. Nothing that comes your way is by accident. Everything that comes to you is for a purpose - either a lesson or a blessing.

Give yourself some credit...
List your current projects and the "wins" you have accomplished along the way.

Project #1
_____

_____

_____

_____

Project #2
_____

_____

_____

_____

Project #3
_____

_____

_____

_____

Project #4
_____

_____

_____

_____

_____

CHAPTER 16

Your Privilege is Showing

Definition of privilege is a special right, advantage or immunity granted or available only to a particular person or group of people. Often, the word is used with a racial connotation. There are other ways the privilege is displayed that has absolutely nothing to do with race. I've experienced that many times over in my professional experience. One situation in particular stands out, not because of the severity, but because of the response when I called the person out on it. He had spoken to someone disrespectfully. When I mentioned it, I was told that that's not what really happened and I heard him incorrectly. I ended the conversation because it wasn't the time nor place. But at that point, I realized his privilege had made him tone deaf. It had made him tone deaf and immune to actually noticing, recognizing and acknowledging his disrespect to another.

There's the privilege you feel when you've been at a company or in a position for a long time. Everybody comes to you for everything and you feel have a certain level of privilege. You feel special and have immunity because you've been at this particular workplace for such a long time. Right? Let me help you with that. And this goes for not just work. This is for organizations, churches, community groups and volunteer organizations. When you start believing that because you've been there a long time or you created it or your name is on the letterhead or you believe "if it wasn't for you, it wouldn't have gotten done," the privilege you walk around with shows up. It shows up in the way that you treat people and how you speak to people. It shows up in the way that you handle situations. For example, you hide behind policies and procedures. You've been there so long; you probably wrote the procedure. Your privilege shows up in a way that you completely dismiss a colleague with fewer years at the company, but who has their own valuable experience. People are aware when your privilege shows up. Your tone changes. Your actions change when you feel threatened by new ideas. Your interactions change and you might look down your nose a little bit. Your privilege shows up when you feel that you have been doing something for so very long that no one should dare question you.

Your privilege is a detriment to the growth of anybody else joining the company, church or organization. When you believe that you have a special right, advantage or immunity granted, you do not allow yourself to be open to hearing other ideas. I remember joining a professional organization and being told very early on that it was a little old ladies club. They don't like anybody coming in ruffling feathers or coming in with new ideas. And sure enough, I watched the dynamic play out. Every single person who had a brand-new idea was shot down because those in leadership positions felt that they had the privilege to tell them that their idea wouldn't work for a myriad of reasons. I've been at workplace where I've seen both sides. I've seen the side where someone has been at the company thirty-plus years and has taken me under their wing to show me how things were done. On the flip side, there were others who were insulted that there might possibly be a better way to address a challenge. When people get well rested in their privilege and "this is who I am" mentality, they completely shut out the possibility of new ideas. Inevitably, something will happen and they will need the very same people they isolated and ostracized with their privilege.

Privilege is not just about race. Privilege is displayed by those who perceive themselves to be better than others. There is always a group in any and every setting: member organizations, the PTA, at work and community organizations, volunteer organizations, etc. Here's what I've noticed. Growth and positivity happen when people choose to share their knowledge as well as welcome new ideas and innovative ways to do things. When those people open up themselves to go beyond, "Well, this is just the way it's been and this is how we decided it's going to be," remarkable things can happen. When you open yourself up and welcome new ideas and new perspectives, the setting will flourish. When there's no flexibility, regardless of the damage, stagnation occurs. There's a repeat of the same conversation year after year during the annual team building activity, retreat, training, *fill in the blank*. It's the same conversation because the same people with privilege are running the same activity the same way for years. It's their comfort level. Here's the thing, there is ZERO growth while being comfortable.

If this hit a nerve, you might be behaving like one of the privileged. I challenge and encourage you to put your privilege and sense of entitlement away and see what happens. I'm willing to bet that the environment will change for the better. There will be less animosity and fewer fake smiles. The spirit of collaboration will show up. Growth and positivity will prevail.

CHAPTER 17

Chaos and Why You Shouldn't Be Bothered by It

Fortunately, but unfortunately, I know a bunch of people who are Type A Overachievers. They're a fabulous bunch of people; and they like to get things done, efficiently and effectively with the least bit of fuss and muss. Here's the unfortunate part. It throws them for a loop when chaos starts to ensue. Not chaos from their lack of planning, but chaos from other people interjecting into a plan that's already underway.

Personal growth has helped me tremendously with this. In my early twenties, someone's last minute demand combined with their lack of involvement or knowledge about a project that I was managing would have made me snap. Twenty years later, it is still very much annoying and upsetting, but I don't let it throw me off my game because, in my mind, the goal is to get my job done. Over the course of my professional career, I've come to understand that chaos will ensue; not because of the lack of planning on my part, but because of the lack of planning or attention of someone else. This lesson rings true no matter the title, company or industry. There will always be something that you are working on and somebody will come in at the 11th hour and say, "Oh, but we need to do this or that. Did you think about this? I think you should..." The 11th hour request will always be there, but when you are very clear about your intentions and what needs to be done, the chaos that is caused by other people become completely insignificant. I'm not saying that it will not irritate you. The chaos that comes around you when you are in the throes of your job or in the midst of completing a task that is not induced by your ineffectiveness to plan, but somebody else's unwillingness to recognize what's already been done is not your concern. You have to stay focused on the task at hand. I find that when you're doing a task that directly impacts someone else, 9 times out of 10, they won't have much to say because they're grateful you're doing the task for them. However, when you are doing a task that impacts a larger scale, it will attract unwanted and unnecessary opinions and chaos will ensue.

How you choose to deal with chaos is completely up to you. Understand the chaos is not about you at that moment. Full transparency, my ego, if I allowed it to get big enough, would go stomping into somebody's office and have a complete hissy fit every time chaos occurs. Experience has taught me to diminish my ego because it's not about me. Guess what? It ain't about you either. It's about the lessons that you have to learn along the way. When chaos happens, allow it to run its course because it has to. You can't stop it midway. When you don't hear from someone or get feedback about something that you're working on, you're inclined to walk around and think that you are the bee's knees and you're the best thing since sliced bread. Take the criticism for what it is. Whatever is true, receive the lesson. Whatever is not, leave it. Remember what I said, only hit dogs holler. There will always be someone to ask if you did something or tell you that you should have done something else.

We live in a society of instant gratification. Thanks to Google, people are able to get immediate answers. We perpetuate chaos when we are continuously trying to appease others. Stop feeding the chaos by trying to be all things to all people. Do what you can, but do it in extraordinary excellence because mediocrity is not an option. When you strive to do your absolute best, that is when your excellence shows. If you walk into any situation saying, well, "I'm just going to do just enough," you perpetuate additional chaos.

Think about all the places where you have strife and agony. Have you ever taken the opportunity to look at the situation for what it is? Did you see what ingredients you might have added to the stew of chaos? Did you take responsibility for the part you played? One of my favorite quotes from Vince Lombardi, a legendary NFL coach, says, "Every job is a self-portrait of the person who did it. Autograph your work with excellence." It is one of my favorite quotes because I don't ever want something that I have completed or was tasked to do to be looked upon as mediocre. Therefore, I'm passionate about every project; and my goal is to complete each one with excellence. That is how I'm able to ignore the chaos.

You might be reading this now and say, "Jesus, be a fence. I do not want to go into work today or tomorrow. There's going to be foolishness and shenanigans." Here's my encouragement to you. Go with the mindset of this job needs to be done. This task needs to be done and it needs to be done in excellence because you are doing it. Forget about who benefits from the completion. Forget about the work that has to be done. Do not think about the complications and annoyances of the day. Shift your mindset and say, "The task that needs to be completed needs to be done in excellence because my name is on it. I'm autographing this." When they look back at the project next week, next month, next year, or the next 10 years, they will see your work and know who spearheaded the initiative to save the company money. They will know it was you who figured out a more efficient process. It's not about the people surrounding you. It's not about the nonsense that they will surely bring to you. I promise you they will. It's about you deciding to sign your name in excellence in the midst of chaos and why you should not be bothered by it.

Nothing will test you more than people who are completely shocked by your capabilities to achieve. Personally, it is a joy for me to watch other people's shock and awe watching other people be absolutely damn fabulous. It gives me fits of giggles. When I hear people say, "Oh, she/he did that?!," I think to myself, "Well, why wouldn't she/he do that?" It gives me all types of joy to see other people get the shock of their life when they see the greatness and excellence in people they had underestimated because they didn't realize what that person had in them. It makes me even happier when I'm able to give people who will do amazing, outstanding, fantastic things, the tools to deal with those who underestimate their greatness. Seeing other people win makes me happy every single day.

It's not about the task. It's not about the people surrounding you. It's about you doing the task in such a way that you sign your name in absolute excellence. That's it, and that's all. Sign your name in excellence in the midst of confusion. Sign your name in excellence and be unbothered by the chaos.

Ayanna T. Castro

CHAPTER 18

Three Lessons Learned From Doing Something New

You can't do it alone. As the project manager for a unicorn project at work, I had the opportunity to also serve as the project lead for one of the biggest public events ever hosted by the company. It was the first time we've ever done such a large event with many different moving pieces. And to be quite honest with you, I was very nervous about doing the event. If you haven't learned by now, I am very transparent about my journey to extraordinary. That being said, while I might have had the vision, there was no way in the world I could have pulled the event off by myself.

I realized I needed three different groups of people around me. I needed the volunteers. The people who assisted with setup, moved things around, greeted the attendees and did errands during the day. I also needed a pit crew. I needed the people who on the drop of a dime would and could take care of an issue (Run to the store? Got it. Deal with the fire marshal? Got it.) The pit crew recognized a crisis in progress and immediately acted on it. Then the most crucial to me on that particular day was life support. The life support are the people who were behind the scenes and knew about the event from my perspective. They knew what gave me heartburn and heartache. They knew all of that and in the midst of everything, they sensed when I was at the point of overwhelmed and over peopled. While the volunteers and pit crew dealt with what the public saw and experience, my life support was crucial for me. They were watchful and helped me through the day. *Did you eat breakfast? Did you eat lunch? Give me whatever you didn't finish for lunch, I'm going to put it at your desk. Did you get a drink? Do you need some water?* My life support told people to leave me alone and to give me five minutes. Life support told the pit crew to tell the volunteers, not to call me on the radio. Life support literally protected me and my energy. You need that. I did not know I needed that, but now having gone through that experience, I realize how very important it is to have those three groups of people.

Murphy's Law still exists and it ain't going nowhere.

Murphy's law still exists and it ain't going nowhere. I don't know who Murphy is. I don't know why he has a chip on his shoulder, but when he shows up, it like he's making up for lost time. When you are doing something new, you have to learn on the fly and roll with the punches. As the project lead for this event, my learning curve was short. There were decisions that I had to make without having a lot of time to come to a final decision. There were choices presented: A or B...but neither of them worked and we ended up with C version 4. Murphy's Law requires ingenuity and flexibility. There's no other way around it.

The other thing is you have to stay positive. I know, it is difficult to walk around with a smile on your face when the score it 10-0 in favor of Murphy's Law. Why is a positive attitude necessary? Because you're in the midst of something that's never been done before. You don't have a frame of reference. But guess what? A year from now, the decisions you make will be a frame of reference for someone else. You have to think about the decisions that you're going to make.

Remain positive and know that Murphy usually brings his annoying girlfriend, Naysayer Nelly. Naysayers will try to convince you that you don't know what you're doing. And because Murphy's Law continues It's easy to start doubting yourself. Check in with your life support, do a gut check, take five minutes and then go finish what has never been done before.

The best lessons learned are learned in discomfort.

Refer back to what I said before about the event, it had never been done before. I didn't have the luxury of reading the previous project manager's close out report to refer to on how to get things done. I didn't have project notes that laid out all the different risks that they assessed and how to mitigate them. The committee didn't have that and most importantly the company didn't have that. What we had to do was to knuckle up, roll with the punches and figure it out along the way. I realized during this process, the hardest lessons are seared into my brain. I will never forget them.

Some of the hardest lessons and best lessons are learned through discomfort. If it's easy, if you keep finding the easy way out and that leads to mediocrity. If you keep seeking the easy way out, you are making the bed and preparing the guest room for mediocrity. Sometimes you have to get into a difficult place, but that is where you learn.

These three lessons can be applied to anything you've never done before. Only this time, you have a frame of reference.

CHAPTER 19

Proximity Doesn't Give You Credibility

During my years of being an administrative assistant, executive assistant, and office manager, I've worked with several senior executives and C-suite executives. What I realized is that a lot of people feel that because they have proximity or an attachment to that person, it automatically gives them credibility.

I would like to call bullshit. Your proximity does not give you credibility. Your proximity gives you an avenue to show why people should consider you to be credible, but it does not automatically make you credible just because you're in that seat or position. Credibility is not automatic because you sit next to them in meetings, accompany them to the meetings or run the meetings in their absence. If you don't have the skillset to back up the position that you're holding, your title does not automatically give you credibility. You still have to knuckle down and do the work. You still have to get your hands dirty.

You still have to get out there and communicate with people and find out what it is that they need. You still have to be a problem solver. You still have to make your own personal relationships. Okay, I realize that I probably hurt someone's feelings. I apologize. I say this from life witness experience, not eyewitness experience. The various positions I've held over the course of my professional career didn't make me. No title or appointment to a position has ever made me. What *makes* me is the fact that I am a phenomenal project manager and event planner. I am strategic and forward thinking. I am people-focused and a task-oriented person. That's who I am. You can put whatever title or appointment next to that. It doesn't matter. I'm still the same person when I walk in the door.

You can be next to important people. You can work for them. You can assist them. Heck, you can even share their vision. You can be partners, but there are always going to be people who are out front and those who are in a supportive role. It is perfectly acceptable to be a support behind the scenes and not shine all the time.

Credibility is something that you have to build on your own. It's almost like saying:

> *"My parents went to Yale, so you know I'm Ivy League blood."* No, no, you did not go to Yale. Your parents went to Yale.

> *"Oh, well you know the vice president closed a fifty-million-dollar deal. So, you know we closed that deal."* No, you did not close that deal. Your vice president closed that deal and you provided support.

Don't claim other people's successes or hard work as your own. It's not your success. Even if you opened the door to provide an opportunity for them to shine and show their talent, you, ma'am/sir, did not do the work. Let them bask in their win. Let somebody else tell them they did a great job without you saying, "Well, you know, if it wasn't for me, you know, blah, blah, blah wouldn't have gotten done."

Here's the other thing to consider, being in close proximity to power should not foster an expectation of entitlement. You are not entitled to anything except for the opportunity to show you are still a badass that brings value:

- Whether the important person is in the room or not
- Whether you have a position/appointment or not
- Whether you are in the room for the "important" meeting or not

I would love for people who are given the opportunity to make great change to realize the best change that they can effect on others is showing that hard work is actually valued. The theatrics of "I'm the (enter a title) and I work for (enter an "important" person) and therefore blah, blah, blah" is a bunch of foolishness and shenanigans. It's okay to say when you don't know something. For example, I can't tell you a whole lot about the technical side of audio and visual for an event, but I know the language the audio and visual people speak; and I respect their profession. Yes, I'm the event planner. Yes, I know the technical terms. I know all that good stuff, but I do not believe for a second that my proximity and knowledge allows me to tell audio and visual technicians how to do their job. My proximity gives me access to learn. My proximity gives me access to new experiences, which then make me better. Does that make sense?

Think about your capabilities. Did your title or proximity to power give them to you? I'm willing to bet neither had anything to do with them. People who depend on their proximity to get credibility often show themselves to be inadequate to take on the responsibility that is bestowed upon them. It lessens the credibility of the person who gave you the position. Do yourself a favor. Make sure you do the work to show that you have the skill set to be where you are.

CHAPTER 20

When Ego Gets In the Way of Common Sense

There are a lot of times where our ego, bravado, knowledge, education, status, title, or letters behind our name give us a false sense of common sense. An office, a title and multiple degrees do not automatically come with common sense. Here's where common sense needs to take over.

Number one, ask for help when you need it, and for what you need. That seems really easy, right? When you are stuck in a place where your ego tells you, "Oh, I got it" and you end up dropping the ball because you didn't, that's when your common sense should have taken over. I'm pretty sure in the midst of it there was somebody saying, "Hey, do you need help?" And you said, "I got it." And you kept saying, "I got it. You've probably said it so much that you no longer get offers; and now you are struggling because your ego won't get out of the way to allow you to ask for help.

Ask for the help you need. Nobody's expecting you to be a superhero. While coordinating a weekend-long state conference for my sorority, I had an amazing young lady who helped me the entire weekend. She stayed so close by my side, she was nearly my shadow. Whenever I said "I need...," she asked, "What can I do for you?" There weren't too many times that I turned around and she didn't say, "What can I help you with?" The younger and less wise me would have continued to say, "I got it." The older me with some life witness experience realized I only had two hands, but had 260 people to take care of and a hotel to communicate with. My ego could have kept me in a place of running around thinking I could have done it all by myself. Commons sense made me thankful for all of the help that was offered.

When help is offered, say thank you because you cannot do it all by yourself. There is no shame in saying, "I need help" or "I need your assistance."

Number two, when you get to a place where you're able to have some sort of influence or you're in a position where you can assist somebody else to move forward, do so. There is no glory in standing in success by yourself. Are you taking other people along with you? Are you reaching back to say, "Hey, come along with me and learn some stuff along the way."? It's great for you to have accomplishments and be in places of influence; but if you're not taking someone who has expressed interest in what you are doing along with you, you are being selfish.

You were placed in a position of influence for a reason. You don't have the influence that you have to keep it to yourself. It is all about giving back. It is about reaching back and bringing somebody along with you to learn and share the experience. There's going to be a day when I'm old and gray and I'm going to be excited and loving the successes made by those who I reached back to bring with me. I'm looking forward to it.

The caveat is you need to be sure the people you're thinking about bringing with you actually want to go and are ready for it. We assume because we're excited to be in the space and have an opportunity that everybody else is excited or prepared about going and that's not the case. Sometimes, you have to have a conversation. Sometimes you have to listen to the little birdie and discern whether or not that person that you are willing to bring with you actually wants to go. The worst thing that can happen is that you take them into the space where they typically would not have access and they damage your reputation. If they have a genuine interest in learning and being in that space, they will act accordingly.

Number three, please and thank you go a long way. We teach our children to say please and thank you. We remind them that our adult friends are not their friends and should be addressed as Ms. or Mr. (Well, at least in some households. You can't call someone who's older than you by their first name without getting a side-eye from the other adults in the room.) I have colleagues that I call Ms. or Mr., even though they have told me not to. My mother's voice is in the back of my head and my Granny is giving me side-eye from heaven. It took some time, but they finally stopped telling me that I didn't have to be formal. I believe in giving respect where respect is due, especially to my elders. In addition, please and thank you go a long way and it should not be reserved for a peer-to-peer relationship. Your ego will trick you into believing that because you have a title, are in management or a higher grade, you no longer have to extend that common courtesy. Take a moment to think about how you would feel if you were on the receiving end of your request. Professionally and personally, I've had to work with various event venues. The one thing all of them will tell you is that my manners are impeccable. *Thank you. Please. I appreciate your assistance.* I genuinely say it because that's who I am. If I arrive on a Thursday, by Saturday, the entire staff will know my name and their level of "What can I do for you?" exceeds what they typically provide. *Do you need some coffee? Sure. I can get that for you. Thank you so much. I appreciate you.* Please and thank you go a long way with people some may think are supposed to be subservient to you. Basic manners can help you accomplish your goals in the midst of chaos. Events are a different type of animal and it can bring out the worst in people. But if I walk into any venue with an attitude, I know my questions, requests, the last-minute changes will most likely be left unanswered.

Further, I don't like when people walk right up to me and just start talking and asking me for stuff. The person asking me for something will more than likely be met with a look that causes them to stop talking and ask, "What's wrong?" I typically respond with, "Hello, how are you? Good morning, good afternoon. How are you doing? Great. Now that we've got those pleasantries out of the way, how can I help you?" Don't walk up to people and start demanding stuff.

Number four, don't just assume that people don't like you. I have had to learn this lesson a few times. I once had a conversation with two people and I told them, "I really just thought you didn't like me so I kept my distance." They looked at me like I was crazy. Their response was, "We didn't know you, but now that we know you, you are cool with us." Don't assume people don't like you. Sometimes, people have to get to know you." I took some time to digest their response and be honest with myself. I know I can be a lot to take in one fell swoop. Sometimes, it takes multiple times to see me, deal with me, and be around me to understand my heart is as big as Texas. I'm loyal to a fault and I'm an empath. But it takes a while for people to be around me to get all of those different nuances. Stop assuming people don't like you. Have the candid conversation. Be vulnerable and transparent. In the same vein, it requires a certain level of vulnerability to ask somebody, "Have I done something to offend you? Have I done something to hurt you?" If somebody comes to you and asks that question, at the very least honor them and their vulnerability to respond and give them an answer. If it's nothing, then tell them they did nothing wrong. But if there is a reason, have that honest and courageous conversation. You don't have to be everybody's best buddy. But when you're working towards a common goal, it is best not to allow your ego to get in the way.

CHAPTER 21

A Few Reminders

Three simple reminders. What folks think about you is none of your business. It's not your responsibility to explain. Stop being scared. So, those are the three things. Let's get into the first one.

The first thing is **what folks think about you is not your business.** Their thoughts will not help elevate you or generate income for you. What people think about you and your journey does not put food on your table or pay your utility bill. What people think is so inconsequential when it comes to the grand scheme of things of your life. Everybody has thoughts and opinions, but neither should intrude upon your progress. Their thoughts should not delay you from doing what it is you were called to do. Their thoughts should not stop you from being brave, taking the next step, and being who you were destined to be. We've all gotten tripped up with our own thoughts of

"What will people think?" I know I have, but honestly, there's only a handful of people that I'm truly concerned about. Some opinions I ignore because I've learned they can often be self-serving. When you start worrying about what people think, you get caught up in the people pleasing trap. What people think about you, it's not your concern. You shouldn't be worried about it.

Number two, **it's not your responsibility to explain your hustle, your grind, your dream, your purpose.** It is not your responsibility to explain any of that. It is not your responsibility to explain why are you getting up at 4:00 in the morning and don't go to bed until after midnight. It is not your responsibility to explain why you work a nine-to-five and then go to a library to do online classes. It's not your responsibility to explain why you walked away from a lucrative six-figure job to pursue your dream. It is not your responsibility to explain why you finally walked away from a situation that you knew was toxic 10 years ago.

It is not your responsibility to explain any decision that you make for your wellbeing, empowerment, improvement or advancement. Why do I say that? Refer back to point one. What people think about you is none of your business. When you are clear about what you want to do and what you have to do (It is so deep and embedded in you that it's not an option, but a must for you.) you don't owe anyone an explanation.

I don't generally explain the "why" behind my hustle. The story behind Work Your Package provides more of a glimpse into the why and the how, but I don't explain it to anyone because it's within me and intertwined in my DNA. I can't separate it from who I am.

Number three, **stop being scared** (refer back to number 1 and 2). Stop being afraid of taking a chance. Stop being afraid of doing what you know you're supposed to do. Stop being afraid of what people think. Stop being afraid to pursue what you've been dreaming about. There are people (maybe even you) with a dream and hope of doing something. They are so excited about it. They can't wait to do it, but they let fear keep them from doing it. Stop being scared.

I promise you, this is all a little bit of tough love. I fuss because I care. I do it because I believe in your potential. Start the blog. Expand your business. Write the damn book already. If you share your dreams with me, I'm going to remind you. I'm going to ask questions. Don't tell me that you have a desire to do something and then sit on it. Do not tell me that there's something that you have in your heart that you want to do. Don't tell me about it, if you don't want a reminder that you need to go ahead and do it. I am the kind of person that sees the possibility in just about anything and everybody.

I told you, I'm annoyingly optimistic.

I can't do pity parties. I give myself about two to three minutes of tearing up and falling out in the ugly cry; and then I have to move on. The summer of 2018, I lost my beloved Rat Terrier, Biggie. He was my furbaby, my first child and therapy dog before I knew therapy dogs exists. A few days before he died, I had a real good, ugly cry to the point that my face was swollen. He was weak and sickly, but I hadn't made the decision or the appointment to have him euthanized. I realized I was being selfish. He was 16 years old and had lived an awesome and fantastic life.

Again, goes back to point number one, what people think about you, doesn't matter. Some people said, "Well, why don't you take them to the vet, see what they can do?" I wasn't going to do that. I had cared for this dog since he was a puppy. It was time for him to go and it was okay. I had made my peace with it. I really didn't have to explain anything to anybody. He was my dog, so I did what was best for him. That evening, I made an appointment to have him euthanized the next day. The following morning, as I was leaving for work, he was limping around. I picked him up, wrapped him up in his favorite blanket and said, "Buddy, you very well may not be here when I get back. I love you. You've been a very good boy."

If you know anything about the Rat Terrier breed, they are stubborn and my Biggie was stubborn to the very end. In my mind, I believe Biggie's last thoughts were, "Nah, hell no. I'm going to go out by my own bootstraps. No, you won't have to watch them give me those needles." And that's what he did. I found him at home, wrapped up in his favorite blanket. He died on his own terms. I was okay because I made peace with my decision prior to even making the appointment. I had a conversation with myself to say, I know I did everything that I could do.

If you know that you're doing all that you can do, go back to one, two, and three.

One. What people think about you is not your problem.

Two. You don't have to explain anything.

Three. Stop being scared to be you.

You are capable of so much more than what you give yourself credit for. Don't sell yourself short. If you apply as much energy into saying "I can" and "I will" as you do in saying "I can't" and "I don't know," I think you would shock yourself on the accomplishments that you make.

Time to give yourself some credit. List your accomplishments from the last 6 months.

_____

_____

_____

_____

_____

_____

_____

_____

_____

_____

_____

_____

_____

_____

_____

_____

_____

_____

CHAPTER 22

Sink or Swim, It's Up to You

Have you heard the story of the man who was on top of the roof and the floodwaters are rising? A boat comes. Helicopter comes. A jet ski comes. He declines all of them because he believes God is going to save him. He ends up drowning and when he gets to heaven he demands to have a conversation with God. "How could you let this happen to me?," he asks. God says, "Dude, I sent you a boat, a helicopter and a jet ski." It leads me back to the thought of sink or swim. It's up to you. And I think some of us get really caught up in the negative connotation about asking for help. But I believe that there are three reasons why folks do not ask for help. It is either a pride, fear or shame.

Pride

Pride announces to the world who you are. It puffs its chest out and gets cocky. *I have a bachelor's degree. I have a master's degree; I have a doctorate degree. I am certified. I sit in the corner office. I have an assistant. I have a staff. I live in one of the wealthiest neighborhoods. I drive this type of car. My children go to this school. I don't ask for help.*

I find the people with the biggest pride are the people who need the most help because when they fall, they come completely undone. Their pride cannot mask their humiliation because they could have asked for help a long time ago, but they chose not to because their pride. They allow their confidence in their things, their title, their net worth to keep them from asking for help. Don't allow your pride to get in the way of you asking for help.

Fear

I don't want to ask for help. What will they think if I asked for help at work? And now they think that I'm not qualified to do my job. What if I asked for help from my spouse? And now they think that I don't love them. Some of this stuff may sound completely irrational to you, but I have heard these excuses before from people who don't ask for help. *Oh, I don't want to ask for help because I don't want to burden anybody. They have enough stuff on their plate.* I'm raising my hand on that last statement. I don't want to burden anybody. I use that line all the time. People around me have enough on their plate. No, I don't want to ask anybody for anything because they have enough stuff to do. If you surround yourself with the right people, you won't have fear about asking for help. Let that sink in for two seconds. Remember I talked about needing a pit crew and life support? If your pit crew and life support are authentic, meaning they're with you 100 percent through the glitter and the gutter, they are not going to be the least bit put out because you're asking for help.

Shame

The last thing that keeps people for asking for help is shame. The shame of it all. Like, *Oh my God, I'm just so embarrassed that I can't figure this out by myself. I can't believe I can't figure it out.*

You are not the first nor will you be the last person unable to figure something out. I had a conversation with someone at work the other day and they asked for my input on something and I gave the analogy of our company being like a big swimming pool. Everybody comes to the pool from different places and we all have our different experiences and backgrounds. Some of us have come from private industry. So we look at things a little bit differently. Some people are homegrown and all they know is our company. Some people came from the military or a government agency. It's a menagerie of folks that work at the company. We all come and get in this big pool. Some of us hold on to the edge of the pool. The edge of the pool signifies your past experience, your past positions and last company that you worked for, the titles and the certifications that you have. Now what? You don't have your past position, your past company, your degrees or certifications or anything to cling to, but you are sinking...fast. You are now at the bottom of the pool. The smart people who adapt, are agile and go with the flow will start waving wildly for help and accept any color life jacket that comes along. And then there's some people who are so very stubborn and rooted in what they know and how they do things that they will sit at the bottom of the pool and refuse the help because they don't like the color of the damn life jacket. (Insert eye roll...here). If you are being offered help and you are in the midst of sinking, whatever you're sinking in, whether you're drowning at work, drowning at home, drowning in your organization, drowning at church or in your relationships...eliminate the pride, the fear and the shame of asking for help.

There's no dishonor in asking for help. None whatsoever. I feel like because we have created this society where independence is celebrated, asking for help is viewed as being weak. We've lost the art of collaboration. We've lost the art of community. My hope for you today, is that you will look at the different areas in your life where you are allowing fear, shame or pride to keep you from asking for the assistance and the help that you need. This goes from the simple: *I need to find a vendor for whatever at work and I'm pretty sure somebody else in my department worked on it* (But I'm not going to ask her because if I asked her then she's going to think I can't do my job.) to the major: *I'm sitting in my house every day hoping and praying that I could find enough strength to get out of bed in the morning. And I don't know how I'm going function throughout the day.*

It's okay to ask for help. Asking for help allows you to grow and growing allows you to help others. It is cyclical. Don't allow your pride, fear or shame to keep the cycle from flowing.

CHAPTER 23

Show Your Scars, Part 2

Some of us have to deal with some heavy issues. Whether it's being a long-distance caregiver for a parent or grandparent, advocating for a child with learning disabilities, having a sick spouse, experiencing infertility, etc., the list can be extensive. How can you flip it around so that your scars can be beneficial for the next person? There are three things that you can do. You can either speak about it, write about it, or volunteer.

Speak About It

There are many different organizations that cater to your type of scar. If you have received help or are actively receiving help, ask the organization if they have a group session for new people. Put yourself back where they are...they are scared beyond belief, they don't know what to do, and their scar is fresh and still bleeding. If the organization has an opportunity for you to speak to people who are new to dealing with what you have dealt with for the last year, three or 10 years, go speak to them. There's nothing more comforting than talking to somebody who has been where you are and has arrived where you are about to go, someone who knows the ups and downs of the experience. This is where life witness experience is golden. When you have a life witness account of a scar, you help people gain a new perspective. You can share how you were able to cope.

When I dealt with infertility, I thought I was the only one and I didn't have anyone to talk to. Some of my girlfriends who had kids before me were very understanding and mindful of the conversations they had with me. Others either lacked empathy or were selfish; and conversations with them added to my feeling that I was the only one suffering. It wasn't until I reached out on an online community that I found out there were women like me who were going through the same exact thing. It was very difficult to be in a certain age bracket and it seems like everyone is getting pregnant, but you. It was one of the hardest periods of my life, but I lived through it and was eventually blessed with two little women. But because of that experience, I am an open book when it comes to infertility, preterm labor, bed rest, cesarean section deliveries, epidurals, cervical cerclages and the effects of too much anesthesia while in the delivery room.

Write About It

If you're not comfortable speaking about it, consider any blogs and newsletters that might have helped you through your issue. Ask if you can be a guest blogger or contribute an article. Better yet, start your own blog. Writing can be therapeutic on so many different levels. There was a time after my oldest daughter was born that I couldn't talk about infertility without tearing up because it was still fresh. By the time I had my second daughter, I realized that my experience might help others and I wrote an article for a magazine dedicated to women struggling with infertility.

Volunteer

I've often said that what I refer to as My Life 2.0 will include me speaking globally. Then, My Life 2.5 will consist of me volunteering at a hospital, specifically the NICU and being a mother's advocate. Thankfully, both of my daughters were born healthy and did not spend any time in the NICU, but I have family members and girlfriends who weren't so lucky. My first delivery was scary. I remember my first 24 hours in the hospital and feeling like I was all by myself even though the nurses were there. I want to be that person that goes to a new mom's room and say, "It's okay if you take a nap, I'll be right here with the baby when you wake up." I want to be that person who give the nurses a break. If you've ever paid attention at a maternity ward, you would understand the nurses often work long shifts. They do their level best to care for all the babies, but many hands make light work. I want to serve as a surrogate warm body to hug and love up on some babies. I want to ease some of the worry of a brand-new mother because she's exhausted from a C-section delivery and her body is fighting against her. If I can take that worry off of her by saying, "It's okay, sweetie. You go ahead and sleep. You take a nap. I got the baby. Don't worry. I'll be right here when you wake up," that would make me happy and my scars will not be in vain.

The other part is I want to plan birthday parties for babies and kids who are in the hospital on their birthday. When one of my brothers turned six years old, he was in the hospital for an emergency surgery to remove his adenoids and tonsils. He spent his birthday in the hospital. My mother was determined to celebrate his birthday despite the hospital bed and his inability to speak for a few days. I can still remember his smile when he saw all the balloons and gifts.

Volunteer at the organizations, missions and places that speak to you. Go to the places that helped you heal. I'm not saying your scar is gone, but if they helped you through that process, go back and give.

I know that it's very difficult for people to want to open up and talk about their scars. I saw a quote that said, "Don't forget to heal yourself before you bleed all over the people who didn't cut you." The ability to show your scars provides you with space to grow and to teach others. It allows you to be more empathetic and helps with your mental health. Your scar is part of your story, but it isn't your personality. Showing your scars doesn't require you to take on the personality of someone who was defeated. It is quite the opposite. It shows how strong you really are.

CHAPTER 24

Don't Let Them Take Advantage of You

This is a touchy topic because the people who are being taken advantage of usually don't realize it and the folks that are taking advantage of people are mad when they get called out on their behavior. I've seen it in my personal and professional lives, but it shows up the same way.

Why do good people allow other people to take advantage of them? When someone helps someone else, and not only is their kindness not reciprocated, but bastardized and taken advantage, I honestly don't know how some people sleep at night. Have you ever seen a situation where someone who's so kind, so good natured, and so well-meaning is taken advantage of by somebody who does nothing but prey on others? They prey on those who they know have a good heart and know will instinctively want to do the right thing by helping someone in need. I'm convinced there's a special place in hell for people that prey on the pure of heart.

But in the meantime and in between time, I need people like me, who love to help and be there for other people, to stop allowing others to take advantage of your kindness. Take a minute to think about the people who are taking advantage of you emotionally, financially, physically, or so many other ways. Think about the people who mooch off you and act entitled to you and what you have to offer. They feel entitled to whatever it is you have. I've said it before, but it bears repeating, **you teach people how to treat you.** If you've allowed the behavior for a long time, you might be saying to yourself, "Well, I can't stop it now. It's been going on for so long." I'm here to tell you that you *can* stop it; and not only can you, you should stop it. The way they're taking advantage of you and your kindness is stopping you from progressing and doing what it is you need to do. You are so busy giving and giving some more, what's left for you? I can tell you what's left, absolutely nothing. Don't allow people who have not sown the seeds and tended to the garden to come by and pluck you for your beautiful flowers or for your delicious fruit.

I'm not saying if you're one of those people that likes to help to turn into somebody who's cold and harsh, but I need you to think about why you continue to be put in a situation where you're being taken advantage of. Don't allow your good nature to keep you from doing what you were called to do. Don't allow the goodness of your heart to keep you from having common sense. Does that make sense?

There are two reasons why we allow people to take advantage of us: we want to be liked or we don't/can't say "no." Did you know that "No" is a complete sentence? It doesn't hurt anybody for you to say "no," but I can tell you it puts the people who were mooching off your goodness on notice and tells them you are paying attention to their foolishness. Saying "no" also helps you take notice of how you don't hear from them unless they need something.

Here are a few ways people are taking advantage of you.

Emotionally: They only call you when they're in despair. There is zero consideration with what is going on your life when they call you. They don't ask if you are busy or even if you have the emotional bandwidth to deal with the conversation. The assumption is when they call, you should drop everything and answer. Here's the problem, they are never there for you in your time of despair.

Financially: When they hear you got a promotion, they hit you up for a loan. When you are at dinner, there's an expectation that you will foot the bill. But...when you are in need, they don't even respond to a text.

Intellectually: "Can I pick your brain?" is an insulting question when you are asking someone to share their intellectual property and expertise. However, folks do it every day with the expectation of getting subject matter expert advice for free. Yet, they can't even lend you an ear to bounce an idea.

Socially: They don't speak to you unless you're around certain people because they want to give the illusion the relationship is stronger than it really is. Let me make this plain for the folks in the back. *Some people are pimping you just for your name and reputation as their entrance into doors that they don't deserve to walk through.* They take advantage of your well-known, stellar reputation and will use your name in such a way that people think, "Oh my, well if they're using a person's name so much, they must have a great relationship with that person." They're dropping your name in certain circles, hoping that it'll give them some influence. Cut off those ties. There's nothing wrong with letting it be known that the person is not as close to you as they would like to imply.

I believe that we are all here to serve others with our special gifts and talents. I also believe that you can't really give if you have someone sucking the energy out of you that should be used for those created to receive what you provide. Think about that for a minute. You were created to provide a gift. There are people who were created to receive what only you can provide. Why? They must receive so they can give something to somebody else. It is a constant flow. You give, they receive. They receive, they give. They give, others receive. That's the way it should flow. But it can't if you have somebody in the middle taking up your time, energy and space being a moocher.

CHAPTER 25

Yes, You Can Be Productive and Not Burn Out

Managing your 168 can be difficult. Managing multiple 168's can be maddening. For the people who manage multiple people and responsibilities, it can all become overwhelming. If you're busy in all of the different facets of your life, the tendency is to take it all on...at one time. Here's how you can still be productive without burning yourself out.

Stop Overextending Yourself

One thing you can do in order to be productive is to stop overextending yourself. We overextend ourselves by saying, "Oh yeah, I can do that or can be on that committee or attend that event." Honey love, you are doing yourself a disservice when you spread yourself thin. When you want to be great at something, you have to be selective in what you choose to do.

As a parent to two girls, one in middle school and the other in high school, I chose to scale back on some of my responsibilities and obligations because I wanted to focus on what is needed to be productive for me and for my family.

Focus on the Happiness Before the Doing

What if you could focus on the happiness of the outcome of what you're doing rather than the monotony and the anguish of the doing? I think that might put you in a better state of mind. In the book *The Happiness Advantage* by Shawn Achor, he talked about happiness and fulfillment as the best predictors for success, not productivity. Not the other way around. Happiness and fulfillment come and then success and productivity. So, you can't be successful and productive, if you're not happy and fulfilled in what you're doing. It makes me happy to take my youngest daughter to dance school because she's following in my footsteps. It makes me happy to take my girls to Girl Scouts because I was also a Girl Scout and I love to see them form their own relationships. It makes me happy to serve on the subcommittees that I serve for my sorority because they're close to my heart. It makes me happy to do the work that I do because it fulfills the left side and the right side of my brain. You have to be happy and fulfilled in order to be productive and successful.

Treat Your Body Well

I struggle with exercising, eating well and getting eight hours of sleep a day...every day. They happen, but not consistently. I don't always exercise. I'll plan my meals for a week or two and then fall off the wagon. Sleep and I, however, don't get along. My mother told me that I've had my days and nights mixed up since I was a baby. The problem is my brain is like a New York City sewer rat...it never stops moving. It's ridiculous, but I'm learning to work with it instead of against it. The nights I can't sleep is when I get the biggest bursts of creative energy. Instead of trying to shut it up, I listen to it and write it down. Clearing my brain helps me get the rest my body needs and deserves. We have a tendency to push ourselves to almost the brink of exhaustion. I don't know when getting only two or three hours of sleep became a badge of honor, but it's nonsense.

Don't Get Sucked Down the Rabbit Hole

Learn to do the right things with downtime so that you don't get sucked down a rabbit hole. Social media is the biggest culprit. Before you know it, you've been pinning to boards, tweeting and double-tapping for an hour. That's time you will never get back and have nothing to show for it. Make the most of your downtime by doing something beneficial, such as taking a walk outside, meditating, writing in your journal or returning a phone call.

Practice Gratitude

If you've made progress, be excited and happy about the progress you've made and don't beat yourself up about the progress you haven't made. The antidote is gratitude. For example, I had a goal of increasing my steps per day. I didn't hit my goal one week and I was disappointed until I looked at the number of flights of stairs I climbed that week. I had forgotten that I made the conscious choice to take the stairs instead of the elevator. Writing a list of gratitude is a great way to use your downtime.

You can still be productive and not burn the candle at both ends. You can still be productive and not wear yourself to the point of sickness. Sometimes, our bodies will scream for rest, but we're hardheaded and we don't listen. Being busy is not productive. Wearing yourself out until you don't recognize who's in the mirror is not productive. Turning into Snappy the Turtle (shout out to @wendymcintyreofficial) and snapping at your family because you ran from the office to home and now you're trying to figure out dinner and homework and everything else is not productive. That is a vicious cycle that leads to exhaustion. Being productive does not require you to wear a cape. Being productive does not require you to show superhuman strength. It does require you to work smart, not hard.

It requires you to take a minute to reassess what's important. You can have tons of things in front of you, but what's important? What will get you closer to your goals? What will contribute to your extraordinary life? Because if it's not contributing, then it's subtracting and then it should probably go. Don't worry, it's not just you. You are not the only person looking at your 168 hours trying to figure out how the hell you are going to get everything done. But you do have to prioritize and realize you can't do it all. In order to be truly productive, sometimes you have to let some things go. Reminders:

- Stop overextending yourself and do less. Say "no" to whatever the "ask" is.
- Focus on your happiness before you focus on productivity.
- Take care of your body.
- Do the right things with your downtime.
- Practice gratitude.

CHAPTER 26

Know Your Worth

In September 2018, there were two athletes that dominated the news and social media. One for taking a knee to acknowledge social injustices against black men, women and children. The other for being too passionate during a match. It didn't matter that she had fought tirelessly for equality for women in sports. In this particular match, she demanded an apology for the referee's behavior and was painted as a brat. What struck me as odd is that men have displayed the same behavior for years and never faced the same scrutiny and disrespect.

The one thing these two athletes had in common is they knew their worth and didn't give a hill of beans what anybody else thought. They were so strong and steadfast in what they knew to be true that no one could tell them any different. When you know what you know, nobody can tell you different or take it away from you. One athlete knew social injustice and didn't care about popular belief. He sacrificed his career for his beliefs. The other knew that she was one of the greatest athletes of all time and has had to fight her entire career to prove it. Both did what they knew to be true. What happened next came as a shock to everyone who discounted them for their beliefs...a marketing campaign that showcased the knowledge of their worth.

Do you know your worth? Are you confident in what you know? Do you allow public persuasion to make you feel like you don't know what you know? If you allow it to, the little birdie will remind you every single day that you know what you know.

Do you know what you bring to the table? Some of you already bought the table, but you sit there doubting yourself. How many of you walk into a room knowing that you have something of value to offer to your family, to your company, to the organizations with who you volunteer? How many of you understand how valuable you are in the grand scheme of things of moving something forward?

One day at work I had a conversation, well more like a venting session, about the greatest gift that any supervisor, manager, or leader could ever get is a staff that is fully vested in the mission and on what needs to be accomplished. There are a lot of managers that must groom everyone from the ground up. When you walk into a space and you have people already on your team, whether you pick them or they were assigned to you, let them show their worth. Allow them to get passionate about what they love based on their life witness experience. When I witness people who get really passionate about stuff with zero skin in the game, I'm prone to roll my eyes. *Go sit down. You are really just throwing a temper tantrum. You're not passionate, you are seeking attention.* The athlete wasn't being a brat; she was being passionate because this was her life experience. She knew what she knew and she knew her worth and she demanded an apology. *You owe me an apology.*

Do not allow anybody to diminish your worth because they're not able capable of recognizing what's before them. Do not allow anybody to diminish who you are based upon their own self-imposed insecurities. Don't allow it. Don't allow someone to talk you out of doing what you know is right for you for fear of you changing when it's all done. Transformation is a beautiful thing. Transformation increases your worth. You can't stay stagnant. You have to continue to learn and expand upon the gifts that you've already been given. You can't expand upon what you don't know. Do you know your skills? Do you know your value to other people? When's the last time you sat down with some people, besides your board of directors, and asked them: What do you think my strengths are? Where do you think I excel? What is your experience when you interact with me?

You are far more valuable than you give yourself credit. You bring more to the table than you think. The table is yours and you are still wondering, "Oh, should I?" Do what you need to do. Don't diminish your value or your worth. Once you know what you know, nobody can take it away from you. It doesn't mean people won't try, but do not second guess yourself. Your life experience is yours. You are valuable and you have a gift to share. Do not be stingy with it. Do not doubt it. Do not downplay it. You are worthy.

Sometimes, you have to see it to believe it. List everything you bring to the table in each facet of your life.

Home/Family	Career
Organizations	**Purpose & Passion**
Bought the Table	**Own the Block**

CHAPTER 27

Benefits of Taking a Hiatus

hi·a·tus /hī'ādəs/ noun
a pause or gap in a sequence, series, or process.
synonyms: pause, break, interval, interruption, suspension,
intermission, interlude, gap, lacuna, lull, rest, respite, breathing
space, time out; recess

When the summer months are upon us, many of us look forward to taking a vacation. Sadly, it might be the only break that we take a year. When you mention hiatus, people tend to think that you are talking about an extended period of time. But do you know there's no predetermined time limit for a hiatus and it doesn't require airfare and hotel accommodations? A hiatus can be as short as five minutes and still be beneficial.

An Opportunity to Breathe and Reassess

Professionals who manage the lives and businesses of others can easily fall into the trap of speeding through the day without taking a moment for themselves. Many focus on achieving the task at hand while managing multiple projects. Kemetia Foley (@adminregendade) has an awesome challenge during the month of April called "Desk Escape" where she encourages everyone to get away from their desks during lunch and walk for thirty minutes. Getting away from your desk doesn't have to wait until lunch. Take a look at your schedule in the morning, or better yet the night before, and block off time to get away from your desk. I tend to take a hiatus later in the afternoon after I've had a day full of meetings and decision making. It helps me think through the outcomes of each meeting as well as solutions to any challenges I might have faced earlier in the day. Taking a well-scheduled moment for yourself to catch your breath and reassess isn't irresponsible, it provides necessary balance in your work day. When you take a moment to reassess, you can ask yourself what really needs to get done and if the tasks on your list benefit the end goal?

Allow Creativity to Stretch Its Legs and New Ideas to be Born

A hiatus allows creativity to stretch its legs and for new ideas to be born. When you take time to think and not be consumed with what everybody else is doing, it gives you time to be creative. It gives you time to come up with new ideas and different ways of doing things. As the program manager for an employee recognition program, there are several tasks that overlap with other events created to encourage employee engagement. When I can't push past a task, shifting to a completely different event or project will often times spark an idea that I can use. When you find yourself looking at the same presentation slides and unable to compose the next bullet point, save and close the document and step away. Even though you aren't physically working on the document, your brain will still think about it; but it now has free-range to come up with a bunch of new ideas without the risk of you quelling it before it can develop.

Allow the ideas to flow without dismissing them. Write them all down. No idea should be thought of as ridiculous. Then, take the time to flush the list out. Take time to give yourself that opportunity to breathe, to reassess, to get your creative ideas out of your head. There are probably several brilliant ideas in your head right now that can't even get out because you have 50 other things in front of it, vying for your attention. What if you just put those 50 other things on the side for a day or two? If it's not mission critical or not a life or death situation, give your brain a break.

Gives You an Opportunity to Come Back Better than Before

Once you've taken a hiatus, whether it was five or thirty minutes, you may actually be excited to get back to the task at hand. No one knows better than you when you need a break. No one knows better than you when you aren't delivering your best because you are burned out. But eventually, your internal feelings will begin to display externally. You, your manager, department and your organization deserve your authentic best effort.

Ayanna T. Castro

CHAPTER 28

When Adults Act Like Children on the Playground

Let me set the stage for you.

Location: The playground

The Players: The bully, the bully's best friend, the innocent bystander, the witnesses, and the grownups.

Bully: The person who pushes other people around. They don't consider other people's feelings and they are a bonafide nuisance.

Bully's Best Friend: The person doesn't want to be a nuisance, but gets enjoyment out of watching others get bullied. They want to put other people in their place and correct them, but they don't want to get their hands dirty.

Innocent Bystander: These people are not directly impacted, but still affected by the bully's and the bully's best friend's shenanigans and foolishness.

Witnesses: The people who see the shenanigans and foolishness going on and say, *"Oh my God, I can't believe this is happening and the adults aren't doing anything!"*

Grownups: The people in charge who are supposed to stop all the shenanigans. They are the people who are supposed to pull the bully aside and check on the innocent bystanders and witnesses to make sure they are okay.

Those are the typical players on the playground. Now, with that analogy in your head, think about the adults you interact with at work, in volunteer organizations, at your children's school or even at church that fit into every one of the roles listed above.

Bullies in the workplace may not threaten you with physical violence, but they often feel it's their right to remind you of what you *should* be doing. They feel the need to "set the record straight" or "put someone in their place." They are typically indignant and stubborn about their opinions. Bullies at work are typically loud and wrong.

The bully's best friend on the other hand, revels in shenanigans and drama, but wants to keep their hands clean because they have a reputation to uphold. They feed the bully information and wait for the fireworks in hopes that it doesn't lead back to them. Well, everybody knows who the bully is and who their best friend is. No one is clueless about their sometimes-tumultuous relationship. You know, they can't stand each other today, but love each other tomorrow. Often, you can trace drama back to the bully's best friend.

The innocent bystander can be anyone. It doesn't matter if you were cool with the bully and their best friend the day before. Anyone can be a victim for a variety of reasons: you disagree with them, you did something they thought you shouldn't/couldn't/wouldn't do, your idea was accepted over theirs, your event was more successful than anticipated, you got a promotion, you took a vacation, you got a new car, etc.

The witnesses are your coworkers, other people within the organization, the other Girl Scout moms, the other cheerleading moms, the other dance moms or even football dads. Witnesses say to each other, "Did you just see what happened?" and they are in complete shock because they can't believe this type of foolishness and tomfoolery is happening in the organization. They are the people who become discouraged because they saw the bullying was unprovoked and, even more so, because it is being allowed to happen.

Finally, there are the grownups who represent leadership. It's the leadership's role to put a stop to the foolishness and shenanigans. Regardless if they were hired, voted in or volunteered, the expectation is that leadership should understand policy and procedures of the organization. They should be able to step in and say, "No, that's not supposed to happen. No, you need to stop that." They are supposed to be the grownups in the situation. What happens when the grownups, a.k.a. leadership, don't step in to protect the innocent bystanders and assure the witnesses that this type of behavior is not only unacceptable, but it will not be tolerated? What happens when the leadership is also in the role of being the bully or the bully's best friend? The morale basically goes in the toilet. You see it on the playground all the time. When kids see that a bully is not corrected, not reprimanded, or even given an excuse for their behavior, they, too, can also become part of the problem. Toxic behavior is contagious.

Have you ever been in a meeting where everything was going great? Ideas were being shared, collaborations were being formed and one person comes into the room and the entire energy of the room shifts. You want to know why? Because everybody in the room knows that person is a bully. Sometimes, the bully does it with a smile on their face and they say, "Well, I just want to make sure that everybody's on the same page." The truth is, they just want to make sure everyone is on *their* page. The bully is sometimes so charming that you don't see the bullying coming until you disagree with them.

So, what do you do if you are the innocent bystander? Well, the first thing you should do is speak up for yourself. Recognize it for what it is and call a thing a thing. Is it possible they will be defensive? Yeah. Should you care? Nope, because no one deserves to be bullied.

What if you're one of the witnesses? Don't be afraid to call people out for their poor behavior, especially if it's against policy or could have legal ramifications.

If you are the grownup, make sure that your actions are always congruent with your words and display ethical behavior, not just when it's convenient. Make sure you're worthy of leadership because people are looking to you to steer the ship. People are looking to you to ensure that things go smoothly. Kids look to adults all the time. *Is everything okay?* And if the adults are not okay, the kids are not okay. Same thing happens in business. We look to leadership to make sure things are okay. When chaos ensues and mayhem shows up, if leadership is not at the helm to take control of it, it causes a toxic environment that can take years to rid. The organization now looks like an emergency room. There are issues in triage, a situation is bleeding out and leadership wants to a band aid on it. The situation requires surgery and stitches, but some leaders are complacent with chaos so there's no urgency to find a solution.

Don't be a witness and not say anything. Don't be in leadership and not worthy of the title you hold. Stop being a bully. Stop being the bully's best friend. I can imagine the power trip feels good knowing you have that type of influence in the room. But please know amid your power trip, you are racking up a body count of innocent bystanders and witnesses who no longer want to be around you, the department, the company, the organization or the church.

Is it really all worth it? The bully would probably say, "Well, if it's really worth it to them, then they would stick it out no matter what." Guess what? Sticking it out no matter what isn't worth your mental or physical health. Sometimes, the paycheck isn't worth it. Sometimes, not even the organization is worth your peace of mind.

If any of this resonates with you or if you saw yourself in any of those descriptions, either say "ouch" or "amen." You have a choice and you can change. Believe it not, sometimes people don't recognize when they're being bullies. They feel righteous in what they believe and say regardless of who it offends. Sometimes, we don't recognize that we are the bully's best friend and our non-action shows complacency with their actions and words. As the innocent bystander, we might have a hard time speaking up for ourselves and it is easier to "go along, to get along." That might be true for a short period of time, but in the long run, how will it impact you? While not directly impacted by the bully, witnesses are often just as affected as the innocent bystander because they've watched the entire situation unfold and it was accepted as the norm. Their loyalty to or faith in the organization ultimately disappears along with their physical presence.

We owe it to each other to think about the energy we bring into any room. We owe it to each to think about the words we speak and the true intention of our actions. If they aren't of good intent, keep them to yourself. If it's not to help somebody else, keep them to yourself. It's to disparage somebody's name or their reputation, keep it to yourself. Remember what you were told as a child, if you don't have something nice to say, keep it to yourself.

CHAPTER 29

Three Habits of Self-Sabotage

There's no easy way to ease into this topic, mainly because it's either going to be an "ouch" or "amen." Depending on where you currently are in your life and goals, it might be both.

1. Negative self-talk

2. Living in the past

3. Lack of ridiculously ambitious goals

Negative Self-Talk

Let me give you this scenario. You have a friend who's really going through a tough time. They went to work and their boss got on their last good nerve. They went home to complete chaos. The PTA president gave them the blues because they arrived late to the meeting. They just had a rough day. Do you tell your good friend, "Well, that's what you get. You should have known better than to show up five minutes late. You should've had that report done." Or do you say, "You know what? You're human. You're allowed to make mistakes. Today was a rough one, but tomorrow will be a better day." I bet it's the latter. So, are you as caring and loving with yourself as you are with others? Are you as sweet and generous with yourself as you are with others? I know people who will go out of their way to do something for others, but when you ask them when's the last time they took a moment just for themselves, they sit there like a deer in headlights. For your information, reading a magazine while waiting for your kids to finish an extracurricular activity doesn't count.

What do you take care of yourself the same way you take care of others? Do you talk to yourself in such a way that you remind yourself that you are just as special as anybody else?

Living in the Past

A few friends from New York and I share a saying, "If 'if' was a fifth, we'd all be drunk." If it didn't happen, why talk about what could have happened if it did? If it did happen, you can't do anything to change it. Regurgitating the same miserable experiences over and over can lead to self-negative talk. It's that negative voice in your head that will remind you of past mistakes, convince you that you can't move forward, and continue the cycle. Why continue to live in the past when you have an entire future in front of you?

It's a self-sabotage to keep yourself in this perpetual loop. Don't continue to write the script of how you think a conversation will go or should have gone. *I'll say this or I should have said that.* Just let it go. I'm not telling you to be foolish and not be mindful with others because as Maya Angelou said, "When people show you who they are the first time, believe them." Trust me, I'm not telling you to ignore that, but what I am telling you is to let that part of the conversation go. You can be mindful of who they are and how they operate and still navigate yourself appropriately. Based off of that, don't relive the entire conversation or experience. We all make mistakes. Holding yourself and others to past mistakes is a barrier that keeps you and them from moving forward into more positive relationships at home or work.

Lack of Ridiculously Ambitious Goals

When's the last time you wrote down something so ridiculously ambitious you had a good laugh at yourself and then said, "But it's possible." Ridiculously ambitious goals get you closer to your purpose, your mission here on Earth more than any external motivation you might receive. Your ridiculously ambitious goals are only ridiculously ambitious if you're not striving for them. However, writing them down isn't enough. There must be a plan and consistent actions to support the goal.

I've shared my ridiculously ambitious goal on several occasions; and each time I say it aloud, it becomes easier to say and believe. Not just because I'm annoyingly optimistic, but because I'm putting in the work to support the goal. Get a goal that makes you excited every time you look at it.

Self-sabotage causes limitation which is akin to mediocrity.

What is the narrative of your negative self-talk?

_____

_____

_____

_____

_____

_____

What scenario are you replaying?

_____

_____

_____

_____

_____

_____

What are your ridiculously ambitious goals?

_____

_____

_____

_____

_____

_____

CHAPTER 30

Transparency

Transparency shows up in different ways and in different places - at home, with your personal board of directors, and at work. While the levels of transparency might be different, it's still a level of vulnerability.

At home, transparency can show by saying, "I need help." Women have a tendency to say, "I got it" a lot. Even when we delegate a task, we are impatient and end up saying "You know what, I'll do it. Otherwise, it won't get done." The problem with that type of thinking and doing is that it gets in the way of saying, "I don't feel well. I'm really tired. I need to rest. Can we get take out instead of me cooking? Can you look after the kids while I take a 20-minute nap?" Transparency at home can lead to an honest and truthful conversation about what really happened in your day. We try to shake off what happens during the day before we get home, but sometimes the residue of the work day lingers and impacts our conversations at home. The good thing is the impact doesn't only have to be from the negative stuff. Sharing the wins of the day can be helpful, too.

With your board of directors, transparency is asking for honest feedback and a request to have your coattails pulled if you aren't living up to your fullest potential. That type of transparency pushes you to want to do and be better. You have a tendency to achieve more when you know you are being held accountable. It also allows you to express that you don't have all of the answers and you need assistance. When you are a maven, it's easy to fall into the trap of thinking that we have to be the subject matter experts in everything. FYI, you are not an expert in all things. Stop frustrating yourself by trying.

There are multiple layers to vulnerability and transparency. The deeper you go, the more it can shake your self-esteem and confidence which is why you have to be selective with whom you share both. However, with the right people, admitting you don't have it all together, you need assistance or you are hurting is not a bad thing. It is part of a necessary growth process.

Transparency at work can be difficult and tricky to navigate depending on your work environment. If you have been working on the same project for two weeks and you are stuck on the first task...there is ZERO shame in asking for assistance. The people who work closely with you will probably see that you are struggling and offer to help. Instead of saying, "I got it,", tell them that you need some time to process everything, but will ask for help when you really need it. I'm speaking from personal experience. I know I can get to the point where I'm overwhelmed and there are people in my life who will jump right in to assist when they see me struggling. I have conversations with them about my need to talk through the problem first before I can ask for help. Without talking through the problem, how am I supposed to properly ask for help? Take time to process your feelings, what you are lacking, what you need, and then go to the people who've offered to help.

Transparency does not equal weakness; it is a milestone of growth.

Where do you need to show more vulnerability and transparency?

_____

_____

_____

_____

_____

_____

_____

_____

_____

_____

_____

_____

_____

_____

_____

_____

_____

_____

_____

_____

CHAPTER 31

Nurturing Your Board of Directors

My definition of a personal board of directors is a group of people who have your best interests at heart. They see your gloriousness and fabulousness. They see your potential and push you beyond what it is that you think that you can handle. They have your back. It is one of the most important relationships you will have with a group of people and it deserves to be nurtured. Your board of directors can come in a myriad of forms. I have both men and women on my board of directors. There are people who are almost twenty years older than me and also two of them being more than ten years younger than me. My board consists of different ethnic, religious, educational and financial backgrounds. It's important to me to have diversity of opinions and life witness experiences.

Are you Speaking the Same Language?

I'm not talking about English, Spanish or Swahili. I'm referring to the lexicon used with everyone. For example, if I call somebody on my board of directors and say, "I need to run something past you" they know I already have something in my head. They know that it's probably fully vetted, but I have to get it out of my head and run it past someone to make sure it makes sense. If I call and I say, "I need you to tell me whether or not I'm crazy" they know I'm coming really close to jumping off the ledge and losing my composure. If I've gotten to the point where I've talked about a situation for too long and I say, "Well, that's it and that's all" they know I'm done with the conversation. We might revisit the topic later, but at that moment, I'm done. This language and understanding have been developed over the years, and sometimes within months, but they understand me and I understand them. You have to make sure you are clear in your communication. An emergency for you might not be an emergency for them. When you are in crisis, you have to say it. I don't push the panic button often because when I do, I know that they're going to respond. If you push the panic button, does your board of directors know the button has been pushed? Are they paying attention to the blinking light above them saying, "Holy crap, they need me ASAP."

Stay Consistent

I have pet names for everyone on my board because I love them. They have special places in my heart and they know it. Thankfully, none of them have voiced they are offended by their names. I have pet names for all of them. I'm consistent with that. They all know that I have a cussing spirit and I tell them to pray for me. I think the prayers are working for my mouth, but my face is a completely different story. I digress. One particular board of director member knows that if I start off my sentence with a slew of some choice words, she already knows it is going to be quite a conversation. She knows to get comfortable because I'm going to have a lot to say before I even get to the heart of the matter. She knows I have to get beyond the emotion before I get to the logic. How am I able to say this which such certainty? She is consistent and not wishy washy with her support. In the same vein, you can't be wishy washy when it comes to the method of how you ask for help. When you're consistent, they know what to expect from you. If they know what to expect from you, they can anticipate your needs a little bit better and vice versa. Pay attention to how they consistently communicate with you.

Help Them Help You

Let them know your current priority. We tend to share a lot stuff with our board of directors. They are the people with whom we share our goals and aspirations. My board of directors knew about my desire to speak internationally long before I announced it to the public. They knew I wanted to get my first book done, get started on the second book, finish my first novel and get some professional certifications. They knew all of the goals, but they also knew my priority at any given point in time. When my priority shifted to obtaining the Project Management Professional certification, we didn't talk about me going to speak in London two days after the exam. We didn't talk about Work Your Package™ at all. The conversation centered around studying for the PMP exam. *Are you prepared? Do you feel comfortable? Do you have your snacks?* All of our conversations circled around the priority at the moment. I passed the exam on a Friday afternoon. On the Saturday evening before leaving for London, the conversation shifted again. *Are you prepared for London? Have you finished packing? Did you run through your presentation?*

Face-to-Face

Make sure you schedule time to have face-to-face interaction. Many of us have members of our board of directors scattered across the globe. Social media has allowed us to be members of a global community. We no longer have to live within a two-block radius of each other anymore to consider each other friends. However, you have to make time for face-to-face conversations. Schedule time for coffee, lunch or dinner. The only thing better is getting all of them in one room. Did you know only seven percent of your message might get across in an email or a text? It increases to thirty percent when you are on the phone. But jumps to fifty-five percent when you are face-to-face.

Nurturing the relationship with your board of directors requires communication, consistency and reciprocation. Don't wait to reach out to them when you are in need. A quick text message to say you are thinking of them and to find out if they are okay is part of nurturing your relationship. Make sure you are speaking the same language; and that might require doing some homework to figure that out. Be consistent with who you are. Let them know your priorities and where you need help. Last but certainly not least, make time to have face-to-face interactions with your folks because nothing beats the conversation and ideas that are sparked when you are in each other's company.

Create a plan to nurture your personal board of directors.

Weekly

_____

_____

_____

_____

_____

_____

_____

Monthly

_____

_____

_____

_____

_____

_____

_____

Quarterly

_____

_____

_____

_____

_____

_____

_____

Annually

_____

_____

_____

_____

_____

_____

_____

CHAPTER 32

Worry About Yourself

wor·ry /'warē/
Verb - give way to anxiety or unease; allow one's mind to dwell
on difficulty or troubles.

Noun - a state of anxiety and uncertainty over actual or
potential problems.

When you hear the word "worry" do you immediately have a negative thought? The problem with the negative connotation around worry is that people tend to think that if they're worrying about something, they're not being productive or if they're worrying they're not trusting God. (Matthew 6:34 - Therefore do not be anxious about tomorrow, for tomorrow will be anxious for itself.) I believe there is some benefit from worrying about some things.

Not all worry is futile and nor is it destructive. A white paper study stated some level of worry is actually beneficial to you. It can actually act as an emotional buffer against things before they come up. For example, I worry about my children's education; therefore, I'm a very active parent at their school. My worry includes talking with their teachers and getting to know the administrators. I worry about my mother because she lives 80 miles away from me. It's not far, but it's not close. I depend on the little birdie to sense if something is wrong with her or my dad. My worry causes me to check in with them on a regular basis.

Worry can also buffer you against some of the disappointments you know will come your way because life isn't always peaches and cream. I am annoyingly optimistic. The house can burn down and I will thank God my family is okay. I'm thankful I have the ability to look at a dire situation and find something positive. But even in my eternal optimism, I still worry; but then I'm not thrown for a loop because, in my mind, I've prepared for almost anything that could happen.

In addition to your little birdie tweeting, "Hello there, something is wrong," worry also confirms you need to pay attention. Worry is not something that you should dismiss, but something you could use to be encouraged to fix whatever is wrong. Are you worried about your health? Talk to your doctor. Concerned about your career path? Create a plan to get you where you want to be.

Worry also shows you are paying attention to details. There are some people who are cavalier about life (if the sun rises and sets, it's a good day) and they don't pay attention to details. An elephant can walk into a room, break the china, sit on the couch, break the couch and the coffee table, and those people wouldn't notice. Meanwhile, the people who worry see the elephant walk in the room and immediately ask, "Why is this elephant in the room?" Then, they go about moving the china, couch and coffee table out of the way so that it doesn't get broken. When you worry, you have more attention to detail and you can be a positive influence because you are able to point out potential pitfalls. Worrying does not have to make you a Debbie Downer or Negative Nelly. It can make you astute to what's going on around you.

Worry teaches you to learn from your past mistakes and works well with the little birdie. The little birdie will remind you: *Remember the last time you touched it, it was hot. Remember the last time you touched it, it was sharp. Remember the last time you talked to that person, you walked away with a headache?* The little birdie and worry go hand in hand to remind you of the negative experiences and allows you to learn from them.

I often tell my girls to worry about themselves when they begin to bicker and argue or find themselves entrenched in the latest school drama. I tell them that so they focus on themselves. That advice works for adults as well. If you are worried about you, you can't focus on anybody else. Worry about your physical health, your mental health, your finances, your career and your life's passion. Stay astute and on top of the details of your goals and aspirations.

Worry about yourself.

What do you <u>need</u> to worry about?

_____

_____

_____

_____

_____

_____

_____

_____

_____

_____

_____

_____

_____

_____

_____

_____

_____

_____

_____

CHAPTER 33

Coach, Mentor, Sponsor, and a Personal Board of Directors? Yes, You Need All of Them.

I truly believe that in order for one to be successful, you need a combination of personal and professional coaches, mentors, sponsors, and a stellar personal board of directors. To date, only one of my mentoring relationships was/is formal. My coaches, mentors and sponsors have been seasoned co-workers and supervisors who embraced that I'm a sponge and love to learn, as well as executives with the power to put me in rooms that I otherwise would not have entered. It is a combination of those relationships that cultivated my ability to communicate and connect with just about anyone and take criticism constructively, no matter how it's delivered. My personal board of directors has evolved over time with some steady members. While there might be some similarities, the roles of a coach, mentor, sponsor and a personal board of directors are quite different.

Coach:

Newsweek reported that a life coach is part consultant, part motivational speaker, part therapist and part rent-a-friend. Coaches work with managers, entrepreneurs, and just plain folks, helping them define and achieve their goals — career, personal, or most often, both. According to *CFO Magazine*, coaches have the ability to view things from afar — in what some call "helicopter vision" — and to shed new light on difficult situations. They often act as a sounding board through tough decisions, help sharpen skills, and motivate. A life coach can help you find clarity when your objective seems vague.

Mentor:

Mentoring is a long-term relationship where the focus is on supporting the growth and development of the mentee. The mentor is a source of wisdom, teaching and support, but not someone who observes and advises on specific actions or behavioral changes in daily work. The Merriam-Webster Online Dictionary defines a mentor as "a trusted counselor or guide." Others expand on that definition by suggesting that a mentor is "someone who is helping you with your career, specific work projects or general life advice out of the goodness of his or her heart. (www.thebalance.com)

Sponsor:

A sponsor is someone in a position of power who uses his or her influence to advocate on your behalf. A sponsor could be your boss, your boss's boss or anyone who's in a position to influence others and who knows you well enough to put his or her reputation on the line for you. That's in contrast to a mentor, who is typically someone who provides advice and helps you develop skills. Mentors help individuals get better, while sponsors help individuals get ahead.

According to Joann M. Eisenhart, Senior Vice President, Human Resources, Facilities and Philanthropy at Northwestern Mutual, there are three facts about sponsorship. First, sponsorship is earned. Only when a person knows your work, trusts you and can attest to your character will he or she likely be an advocate for you. Most won't risk their own reputation on anything less. Second, sponsorship doesn't have to be formal. Because sponsorships are based on professional relationships that are cultivated over time, they often develop informally. Years ago, I was offered a position at a new company because a former colleague suggested the hiring manager get to know me. My colleague and I never said, "Let's be sponsors for each other." Instead, the recommendation came as a natural extension of our strong professional relationship. Lastly, sponsorships are two-way streets. If you're fortunate enough to have a professional sponsor stick his or her neck out for you, please don't disappoint. In return for their advocacy, they'll expect you to live up to your potential. And they may ask you to work on aspects of your career development before they're willing to go to bat for you. After all, their credibility is riding on your success.

Board of Directors:

A board of directors can go by many names: "inner circle", "advisory board" or the newest buzzword your "squad." Are you sure you have the right members on your personal board of directors? Here are some questions to consider:

- Are you surrounded by people who push you towards being extraordinary? Or are they okay with you settling for mediocrity?
- Do they challenge you? If you aren't sure if they are challenging you, think about how many times they have asked the simple question, "Why?" You know, I was thinking about getting my doctorate. Why? I want to start a blog. Why? I am really thinking about switching jobs. Why? They aren't asking "why?" to discourage you. They are asking so that you can hear your own answer. Sometimes, we have great ideas in our head, but when we begin to talk about them in detail, we realize the idea isn't great after all. They help you think through ideas before you make a decision.
- Do they support you? Do they show up? Do they encourage you even when you are terrified because they have confidence in what you have to offer? Are they your brand ambassadors? Do they tell other people about how awesome you are?
  Do they expand on your ideas by saying, "Yes and did you also think about..."
- Do they allow you to vent, but keep it from becoming a pity party? Are they your "10-minute person?" A 10-minute person is someone you can call when you just need to let out some frustration and vent. For those 10 minutes, the job of the other person is to listen, not to comment, not to add fuel to the fire or offer solutions to

your problems. At 9 minutes and 59 seconds, that person should stop you by saying, "Okay. Do you feel better getting that out? Great. Now what are you going to do about it?"

- Do they have dreams and aspirations of their own? You may be thinking, why is that important? Well, when you are surrounded with people who are just as eager as you are to be extraordinary, it leaves no room for jealousy and opens the possibility for collaboration.

Your board should be eclectic with various backgrounds, educational levels, professions, interests and passions. Embrace having both men and women with a broad spectrum of ages on your board so that you can benefit from different perspectives on any challenge you may face.

Take an inventory of who surrounds you. Some of the qualities a stellar personal board of directors include:

- The consistently have your best interests at heart without having a hidden agenda.
- They support you when you want to give up.
- They introduce you to people who can propel you to the next level of your journey, whether it be professionally or personally.
- They are not judgmental and give constructive feedback, not criticism.
- They are genuine with their intent when they offer to help you. Learn how to accept their help and say "thank you." While you might be awesome and amazing 99% of the time, it's okay to not be a superhero once in a while.
- They are not bobbleheads. They are not "yes" women and men. There will be times they will disagree with you. They might remind you of a goal you set and have

conveniently forgotten. When a member of your board calls you out for being on social media instead of studying, spending frivolously when you should be saving, or reminds you to pray instead of complaining, do not get mad. Thank them for wanting the best for you.

Here's the truth about having a personal board of directors. The table will not always be full. When a seat is vacant, it is your turn to sit on their board and support them. You have to be open to having a mutually beneficial relationship; and it's not about keeping score. If you are keeping score, then it isn't authentic and it will not last.

So, do you have a coach, a mentor, a sponsor and personal board of directors? If not, think about the people around who can step into those roles. Who do you go to for advice? Who do you go to when you need clarity on how to get a task or a project done? Who do you know who is where you want to be and has the gravitas to introduce you to the right people? Take the time to talk to them. Find out if you have similarities and are compatible. Find out how you can assist them before asking them to help you. Make it a win-win situation for everyone.

This content first appeared in Executive Secretary Magazine.

Ayanna T. Castro

ACKNOWLEDGMENTS

To my family – Your unwavering love and support make it possible for me to do what I do. Thank you for having my back and providing common sense when my optimism takes over.

To my Board of Directors – There have been days when I just wanted to throw in the towel and then one of you would call, text or email me and give me a laugh, encouragement or swift kick in the butt. You keep me on point and focused on the goal. Thank you for being able to pivot when priorities shift and for covering my back and side.

To the Maven Network – It is an honor to be among such an incredibly diverse group of women. Amazing things continue to happen because we support each other.

ABOUT THE AUTHOR

Ayanna Castro is an international speaker and author and an expert on helping others overcome self-imposed obstacles while in pursuit of their goals. She is the Founder and Chief Maven of Work Your Package™. Her mission is to educate, encourage and equip others from all walks of life to enhance what they already have to become the "total package" and be extraordinary.

Ayanna's inspiring, truthful and transparent approach has made her the "unconventional" member on her client's personal board of directors. Known for having the perfect balance between guidance and support, she is the person women and men call on before they start a new venture or have lost clarity on their goals. As a speaker, she has delighted and engaged various audiences with her message of perseverance and "working their package". Her clients include International Association of Administrative Professionals, Executive Secretary LIVE and the United States Department of the Navy.

Ayanna has degrees in Deviant Behavior and Social Control and Business Administration. She is a Project Management Professional (PMP), certified by Project Management Institute (PMI), a Certified Government Meeting Professional (CGMP) by The Society of Government Meeting Professionals as well as a Certified Administrative Professional - Organizational Management from the International Association of Administrative Professionals (IAAP). Ayanna has over 25 years of professional experience in various industries such city government, law, public relations, private equity, utilities, and media.

Contact Information:
Ayanna T. Castro, PMP, CGMP, CAP, OP
Email: ayanna@ayannacastro.com
Phone: (240) 712-4630
Twitter: @WorkYourPackage
Facebook: https://www.facebook.com/workyourpackage/
LinkedIn: https://www.linkedin.com/in/ayannacastro/

Made in the
USA
Middletown, DE